CW00665746

UNDERSTANDING ACCOUNTING
FOR SMALL BUSINESSES

An essential guide to business finance, accounts, and financial jargon

Andrew Scowcroft

ONION CUSTARD PUBLISHING LTD

Understanding Business Accounting
An essential guide to business finance, accounts, and financial
jargon

© 2015 Andrew Scowcroft

British Library Cataloguing in Publication Data. A catalogue record
for this book is available from the British Library.

Published in the United Kingdom by Onion Custard, UK.

www.onioncustard.com,
Twitter @onioncustard,
facebook.com/OnionCustardPublishing

Paperback format: ISBN: 978-1-909129-658

First Edition: July, 2015
Category: Business / Finance

Table of Contents

Acknowledgements

All authors need a good team around them to turn what is in their head into something that is both accurate and easy to read. Without the help of some pretty special people this book would not have existed and I am only too happy to mark their contributions.

First, I am deeply indebted to Simon Brooks of *Penhow Bean Counters Ltd*, an accounting, taxation and business advice practice based in South East Wales, for his advice on the technical accuracy of the book. Simon's help in identifying the different tax arrangements for sole traders and limited companies was especially valuable.

www.penhowbeancounters.co.uk

Next, to Max Woodman of *Working Capital Partners* for his advice on the different forms of invoice financing. This area was quite new to me and Max provided welcome clarity.

www.workingcapitalpartners.co.uk

To Richard Sugarman of *Go Commercial Finance Ltd*, for his reassurance that my explanation of alternative financing options such as peer to peer and peer to business lending was 'spot on'.

www.gocommercialfinance.co.uk

Acknowledgements

To Rachel Sestini for casting her expert eyes over the manuscript, and applying her considerable expertise.

www.sestiniandco.co.uk

To David Norrington and the team at *Onion Custard Publishing Ltd*, for vital support services, ranging from strong tea and gentle nudging, through to constructive comment on both the idea and content of the book.

www.onioncustard.com

To all my friends and business associates within *4Networking*, for their encouragement to write this book and for their tentative promises to buy a copy when it comes out. I'll be checking the sales figures!

www.4networking.biz

To Julie Faria and Linda Galloway of *April Training Ltd* for permission to use reports from their business simulation software in Part 5.

www.trainingsimulations.com

Finally, to my family for their continued patience whilst I did 'a little more work on the book' and for their unerring ability to spot that howling typo I should have seen for myself

About the Author

Andrew Scowcroft has run his own training and consultancy business since 2001, specialising in leadership development and business management. This is his fourth management book; the first three covering managing people, influencing skills and presenting with confidence. He has also published a travel book reflecting on the culture clashes he experiences during his regular business trips to India.

Andrew lives and works in South Wales.

Introduction

Business owners need good accountants. In return accountants deserve to have good business owners. By 'good' I mean well informed, committed to the task, and willing to listen. The only problem is that the language and terms used in the world of finance can often get in the way of the relationship.

Every trade or profession has its own ways, processes and rituals and that is normally a *good* thing as it gives the members identity and status. As a consequence, every profession also has its own jargon and that too can be a good thing. It provides a shorthand when having speedy discussions between members. However, the very thing that binds professionals together often has the opposite effect; when it comes to business finance it can leave everyone else, including you, feeling left out of one of the most important things in your life – your own business!

If you are smart you will make sure that your business books are kept up to date, either by using in-house systems or paying a professional bookkeeper to keep you on the straight and narrow. The business will probably also need good accountancy support, firstly to give on-going advice, and secondly to make sure that all of the statutory accounts are compiled and submitted to the proper authorities on time.

However, for some business owners that is not enough. They want to know the basics of what their business accounts look like, how they are compiled, what goes where, and what it all actually *means*.

It is for these business owners that this book has been written. It is the book I wish someone had written and handed to me when I started out.

Armed with the knowledge and terms explained, business owners will be able to have more equal and productive conversations with their accountant, and will therefore be better placed to actively manage their business on a day-to-day basis.

How to Use this Book

This is not a completely comprehensive guide to the whole process of setting up a business – from idea, plan, approaching the bank, finding premises, making profits, etc., through to retiring to a chateau in the south of France. I am assuming that advice on these issues has either already been sought, or you have some handy expert waiting in the wings who will help you.

Instead, this book will look at five specific areas, four of which contain critical financial information for the business owner, wherever they are in their journey. The fifth part will give you an opportunity to use your new knowledge to interrogate a full set of accounts and see the connections between the different elements. You will then be able to ask the right questions of the experts you meet, and really feel on top of your business.

The five sections in this book are:

- Part 1: Getting your Hands on the Money - Eight Sources of Business Finance, their features and implications, split between three broad headings.

- Part 2: Business Finance Jargon Buster – what the common terms mean (in language you can understand).

- Part 3: Improving Profits – how to do this and where to concentrate your efforts

- Part 4: Business Accounts - what they contain, what they mean… and why they come in threes!

- Part 5: Advanced Case Study - Analysing Company Accounts

**This book does not constitute legal advice –
please ensure you get current, professional guidance
before making business decisions.**

Types of Business

I will be covering two of the most common types of small and medium enterprise businesses (SMEs) in this book, namely *sole trader* businesses and *limited companies*.

There are other types - such as Limited Liability Partnerships (LLPs) and Community Interest Companies (CICs), and your accountant will help you to decide which is best for your circumstances. Most of the principles of business finance included in this book are relevant across all types of business, but there are a couple of important distinctions to be made between the two I have chosen.

The example accounts provided as a case study in Part 5 of the book actually represent a third form - the public limited company. This is because it offers the chance to look at, and learn how to interrogate, more complex accounts. Once you can navigate your way through those, then working with smaller business accounts should be a piece of cake!

Type A: Sole Trader

If you set up in business as a sole trader, you and that business are one and the same thing in law. You maintain complete control over the business, keeping all the profits after tax. The fact that the law will not distinguish between you as an individual, and your business, means that if the business runs into trouble, you will bear all the legal and financial responsibility.

Sole trader profits are reported on your personal self-assessment tax return and taxed as 'trading income'. Tax on trading income is paid in two installments (on 1st January and 31st July each year). There can be significant tax advantages in being a sole trader and having business profits taxed as trading income as opposed to employment income under PAYE where the amounts allowable against tax are far more restricted. After deducting allowable costs the taxable profit is taxed in a similar way to other non- savings income.

The legal complexities of a sole trader business are fewer as the forms tend to be less onerous and the penalties for missing submission deadlines are less costly. In addition, the cost of an accountant preparing a sole trader's end of year accounts is likely to be lower than for a limited company.

Type B: Limited Company (Ltd)

A limited company is a separate legal entity to its owners, directors, shareholders, and this limits their liability if the business runs into trouble. The normal rule is that the directors' liabilities extend to the amount of their financial stake, so owning £100 of shares means that the normal liability is no greater than £100. Please note that in the event that a limited company takes out a loan, the directors will also be liable for personally guarantecing that debt.

Setting up as a limited company could be more tax-efficient for some people; the profits belong to the company rather than you so, as owner, you could split your remuneration into two types – employee salary and shareholder dividend payments. This could, dependent on current tax rules and expert advice, allow you to reduce the directly employed salary element to fit within a lower PAYE tax band.

Setting up a limited company is likely to be costlier and it requires more ongoing administration than registering as a sole trader. For example, you have to keep records of 'board' meetings and agreements so that significant decisions are recorded but, in the long term, it offers less of a risk to your personal assets if things go wrong than the sole trader option.

The distinction between these two forms of trading is important when it comes to seeking funds (to start or grow the business) and when attracting clients. Some advisors will tell you that being a limited company carries more credibility and stability in the eyes of potential funders, even going as far as suggesting that it conveys a more professional and serious approach to business. There is also some anecdotal evidence that potential clients, particularly major companies and large public sector bodies, look upon a limited company more favourably than they would on a sole trader.

When large companies contract for individual services they generally prefer to do it through a limited company as the client company will be liable for any PAYE due as a result of their subcontractor wrongly claiming self-employed status.

Despite this, many sole traders do very well in highly competitive markets and often form alliances with other sole traders. This means that when bidding for major pieces of work or demonstrating sufficient capacity to deliver a large work programme, they can put forward a substantial consortium bid and appear larger than they are.

The business costs associated with sole trader status – accountancy fees, statutory returns, etc., tend to be lower than those for limited companies, due mainly to the fact that no accounts need to be submitted for a sole trader. There is a breakdown of items required on the self-assessment tax return but this is for HMRC purposes only.

A company does need to send its accounts every year to the Registrar of Companies for public view. However, a small company has the option of submitting an abbreviated set of accounts (primarily just the balance sheet and notes).

Sole trader status normally denotes a single person but that is not always the case. Please take advice from a lawyer or accountant if you wish to run a sole trader business with another person as there will need to be a legal partnership agreement in place to deal with issues such as the distribution of profits, how to cover debts, decision making, dividing the business in the event of a separation, etc.

This book is not designed to discuss the arguments for and against any of the legal forms available as advice is easily obtained locally if you are undecided. Suffice to say that it is essentially a three-way trade off between cost, security and market presence. Ultimately only the business owner can decide which is best for their type of business, given their location, the preferences of their customers and their personal approach to risk and reward. It is common for small businesses to start as sole traders and then to move to limited company status later, but there are no hard and fast rules on this. Check with your current or proposed accountant to discuss the options (including the Limited Liability Partnership option) before making a firm decision.

Part 1:
Getting Your Hands on the Money – Sources of Finance

The first thing to say about financing a business is that *you often need more than you originally thought*, particularly at the start. Of course there are well publicised examples of entrepreneurs who started with nothing and built an empire; I salute them for beating the trend.

Most of us with a business idea need an injection of cash to get things moving. Manufacturing companies will have unavoidable requirements for big machinery, and this needs to be acquired first, either by purchasing or by renting/leasing, whereas a high-tech company may need to invest in some serious research and development activity before bringing a new product to market. Even a retail company will need stock and premises before they can open the doors to the public.

Whichever set up route is taken, and unless there are benevolent customers sitting there offering to pay in advance of getting a product from your company, **money**

will flow out before it flows in. You must make sure this is taken into account when developing your business plan and income/expenditure forecasts. Furthermore, remember that these are not just theoretical forecasts. If you need to make a living quickly from your business, the cost of your own remuneration will need to be factored in. In my case it took 3 months from starting the business until the point when the income from clients was enough to cover a salary for me. Until that point I had two choices – go hungry or ensure that I hade enough start up cash to meet my business and personal needs.

Those whose job it is to provide finance to new or expanding companies will not say "yes" to a business plan that is unrealistic, however good the underlying idea might be. Even if you return to them with revised figures and a better plan, remember the other person is human and probably won't simply forget that you brought a leaky plan last time. They will scrutinise the new figures even more thoroughly. So, it makes sense to get the plan right the first time.

The second big message at this stage is that **not all money is the same**. Some forms of money costs more to get your hands on than others, some will come with conditions, some will carry risks, and others won't. I will highlight the costs and risks as we compare the various sources of funding.

In this section of the book I outline eight main sources of finance for small businesses, some of which have further sub categories. I have separated these eight sources into three different types, namely:

1. **External Sources**
   - Equity, including
     - o Owners equity
     - o External shares
   - Loans, including
     - o Bank loans
     - o Peer to Peer and business lending
   - Crowd funding
   - Grants

External funding comes from individuals and institutions that are neither customers nor suppliers. Therefore their decision to commit funds is not a direct consequence of the trading activity carried out within the company, but more a statement of their broad support for your enterprise. This might affect how you go about persuading them to part with the cash you need.

2. **Cash Flow**
   - Overdrafts
   - Interest
   - Invoice financing

Cash flow is the consequence of how well the company manages the cash coming into it, or leaving it, regardless of the income sources or expenditure purposes.

3. **Trading**
   - Sales revenue

Trading is generated by the products and services offered for sale by the company.

There will always be some people that say that a list like this doesn't cover their particular circumstances or business, but I think I have covered most of the bases -

certainly enough to get you thinking, which is the objective of the exercise.

I have separated them to emphasise their differences and to prevent new business owners from confusing trading income with other forms.

Now, let's look at each source in more detail.

1. External Sources

Equity

If you own a house and the amount you owe on your mortgage is less than its current value, the mortgage folk will tell you that you have equity in that property (a 'stake', or money left over if you were to sell it). The house itself is in your name but its value is divided between the amount that the mortgage company wants back and the balance, which belongs to you.

When the housing market goes south, many people find themselves in *negative equity*. This means that the current value of the property is less than the amount of mortgage secured on it and, if it were sold at that lower value, the owner would have to make up the difference so that the mortgage company could be repaid in full. In short, the lender has priority over you.

In business the word *equity* has a similar meaning. You may be setting up your own business because of a cash windfall; for example you were made redundant from a previous job, you took early retirement, received an inheritance, or have access to other savings. In other words you have a pot of cash standing by – that's equity.

Let's say you open a business bank account and deposit £10,000. That means that you now have personal, or **Owner's Equity**, of £10,000 in the company. Assuming that you are the sole owner of this business we can also say that you have 100% ownership, whereas, if you started the business with a partner who also put in £10,000 you would have 50% ownership of a company worth £20,000.

Equity means that you have a stake in the business. It is your money and, as long as the bank balance is healthy enough and it wouldn't damage the business to do this, you could take some or all of that money out and use it as you wish. But why would budding entrepreneurs want to put their own money into a business in this way?

It can be argued that this is one of the cheapest forms of finance for the business. It is almost like an interest free loan[1], there are no forms to fill in, no proposals to put to a bank manager, and no deadlines or legal conditions relating to how the money is used or when it has to be repaid. So, cheaper and less legally binding perhaps, but is it the obvious choice? Not necessarily.

It can be easy sometimes for a fledgling business owner's enthusiasm for their new venture to get in the way of prudent financial management. You need to be confident that the money will be well used and that it is being put into a business that is likely to make sufficient profits within a reasonable timescale, otherwise the investment is unwise.

At the time of writing, the interest paid to savers by banks in the UK is very low, caused mainly by the financial crisis of 2008 and the double dip recession that followed. However, putting money into a bank account, even a low interest bearing one, is a relatively safe option. Our £10,000, put in an account offering 1% interest per

---

[1] I say interest free but that needs clarification. The person putting equity into the company will invariably expect a higher return over the long term than they could get by depositing the money in traditional savings accounts. However, and this is key, they cannot demand such a return or use the law to secure a minimum return. There is always a risk of little or no return so, using my layman's definition of 'interest' (a fixed and agreed payment in return for the loaning of funds to another party), equity is free of such interest.

year may only have grown to £10,510 by the end of 5 years, and it may not have kept pace with inflation, but that £510 return before tax is certainly better than putting it under the bed or putting it into a poor business and losing everything.

The last thing I want to do is dampen genuine enthusiasm. If you have a great idea, have checked it out with people who know, done some market research and have the backing of those around you, then go for it. But, if you just get carried away and put your life savings eggs into one poorly constructed basket you may have some explaining to do later around the family dinner table!

So far we have talked about owner's equity, the personal funds put in by an individual who wants to run their own company and has some cash to inject. This is the typical sole trader scenario and, in law, the business and the owner are treated as one entity. That means the debts of the company are the debts of the individual, and any profits are taxed through self-assessment. Employees are taxed through Pay As You Earn (PAYE), and National Insurance (NI) for the self-employed is paid by weekly or monthly direct payments.

The second type of equity is Share Equity (often called Investor's Equity). Some companies start out as sole trader entities and then become a limited company, whilst others go straight for limited company status. If you want to be part of a limited company you will have to buy, allocate, or be allocated, a share of that company. This need not be expensive. My own business is a limited company, has two directors who each invested £50 in shares with a value of £1 per share. Therefore we own 50 shares each and so the company started with **Investor's Equity** of £100. In financial speak that also means the company had a *net worth* of £100 when it started.

In this case the amount invested is much smaller than the major cash injection made by our imaginary sole trader but the principle is the same. We have equity in the business and we expect the business to grow so that the value of that equity will increase as profits are added to the original investment.

Given my comments earlier about the low interest rates offered by banks we hope that the business will grow by far more than say 1% per year; otherwise it might have been safer, and less stressful, to just keep our £100 in the bank.

Equity is partial or full ownership of the business, expressed as a financial value, with Owners Equity and Investor's Equity being the two common forms. As the business develops equity will include any initial investment and the accumulated net profits generated by the business. You may see this figure showing on your company accounts as *Total Shareholder Funds*. For example, a company that started with £100 of investors' equity and posted £3,000 in net profits at the end of its first year of trading will have a total Shareholder Funds value of £3,100 showing in its final accounts.

Remember this principle as we will return to it when comparing the cost of equity and the cost of borrowing.

Before moving on it is worth reminding you that any equity invested in the business, either at the start or once underway, carries risk. If all goes well the value of the equity will increase, as in the example above. If things go wrong and the business fails then the owner, or the shareholders in the case of a limited company, will have little legal protection. The money has gone. That's why all investment opportunities will come with a health warning that *"The value of your investments may go up or down, and you may not get back the amount you invested"*.

Loans

The second source of finance is a loan. Traditionally business loans have come from established financial institutions such as high street banks and, if their marketing material is to be believed, they are still open for business. However the 2008-13 recession has led to businesses reporting a widespread unwillingness on the part of banks to lend money to businesses, despite UK government financial help and exhortations to do so. This situation has led to an emerging alternative lending market known as Peer to Peer Lending, or P2P.

In a moment I will explain the main differences between traditional bank loans and P2P loans, but firstly a few comments on the *concept* of a business loan.

Like a personal loan that you might take out to fund some DIY around the house or to buy a new car, a business loan will have some of the same features:

- An amount to be borrowed
- An agreed period over which it will be repaid
- An amount of interest that will be charged by the lender
- The business manager at the bank will want to check that your idea is sound, that your projections of income and costs are sensible, and that you will be able to pay back the loan within the specified time

Let's assume you want a £10,000 loan from the bank to help you buy some essential equipment. This may be in addition to any owners' equity, or it might be an alternative to using your own money.

To keep the figures simple, let's assume that the bank will offer the loan for 5 years at a rate of 10%, on a *capital and interest* basis. That means that every payment you make includes part of the original sum borrowed and a proportion of the interest. Ten percent may sound like quite a high rate, but this is just for illustration purposes, plus evidence suggests that loans for start up businesses *are* typically in the range 8-10%.

That means that:

- You will pay back just over £212 per month
- Each year you will pay around £550 in interest
- At the end of 5 years you will have paid back the original capital sum of £10,000 plus interest of just under £2,750

Some larger business loans are structured so that you only have to pay the interest on a regular basis and can choose to pay back the original sum (the *capital*) at any time and in any amount, as long as the total loan is settled by the original deadline. This is similar to an interest only mortgage that you might have on your home or on any buy-to-let investment properties.

For most small businesses the banks will just offer a straightforward capital and interest loan over a fixed term. In some cases there may also be a set up or arrangement fee added to the loan value, and this can either be paid at the start or wrapped up in the monthly payments.

Cost of Borrowing

Compared to the £10,000 equity example, where you or another investor simply hands over the cash, you can see that a bank loan costs *additional* money to take out (i.e., set up fee, interest, etc.) and that cash will physically leave the business on a regular basis to repay that loan, regardless of what you are actually doing with the money you borrowed.

Those additional costs are known as *servicing the debt*, or the *cost of borrowing*. The cost of servicing your debt is treated as a business expense; it will show up in your business accounts and will be deducted from your operating profits before your net profit figure is calculated. See Part 2 for more explanation of these different profit terms.

Legalities

Unlike equity investment, loans will be accompanied by a legal repayment agreement. Even if the business fails, the bank will be entitled to have its money back, and will no doubt pursue you for recovery of that debt if you default on the payments. The bank can usually do this with a limited company, even if the amount of directors' liability is less than the loan amount because, as part of the conditions for granting the loan to a company, they will seek personal guarantees from those directors. This can be serious, so make sure your business plan is well-founded before you go anywhere near a bank (or any other lender for that matter).

For sole traders, it's even simpler. The owner owes the bank the money and can have their personal assets targeted as the lender seeks to get paid. Some businesses that own assets such as buildings and equipment may be able to use the value of those assets to secure a loan or, in extreme cases, dispose of those assets in order to make repayments.

Loan vs Equity

Assuming you could access both equity and debt (a loan) what are the advantages of each one, and how can you decide which is the best for you?

Here is a simple comparison (ignoring the impact of company tax, just to keep things clear).

Equity Option

I receive £4,000 equity investment from an acquaintance, which adds to my own investment of £6,000. This now means that my acquaintance owns a 40% stake in a business worth £10,000.[2]

If we assume that the business thrives and it posts a retained profit (see Part 2 for a definition) of £10,000 at the end of year 1, this profit is added to the initial £10,000 equity making the company now worth £20,000. 40% of that increased worth belongs to the other equity holder, so his share is now worth £8,000 and mine is worth £12,000. Happy days!

Loan Option

Now, let's assume that instead of securing equity I go to the bank for the extra £4,000 I need. The bank offers me that money at an interest rate of 10%, but is cautious and so wants full repayment within the first year. Excluding any fees, I will therefore pay the bank £400 in interest (i.e., 10% of £4,000).[3]

Again, let's say that the business thrives and ends the year with a profit of £9,600 (the same £10,000 profit as before, but minus the £400 interest payments). Once we pay back the capital value of the loan (£4,000) the company's worth has risen from £10,000 to £15,600, an increase of £5,600. Now for the important message - I own all of that £15,600, £3,600 more than if I had taken an equity partner instead.

The difference between these two scenarios demonstrates the concept of *gearing*[4]. In the second scenario I have leveraged or geared the bank loan of £4,000 into good profits, knowing that regardless of the

---

[2] The only reason I made my own equity greater is so that I can demonstrate the concept of a majority, or controlling, stake in the company.

[3] Note that the bank has no intellectual stake in the business or its growth and no legal ownership of my company or its worth. Theirs is strictly a contractual arrangement requiring repayment of the money they lent plus the interest.

[4] also known in the USA as *leverage*

amount of profit I make I will never owe the bank more than £4,400. With an equity investor their stake rises (or falls) *in direct proportion* to the value of the company, so they own a slice of the growth, which of course is why they would choose to invest in the first place!

Based on these figures, why would anyone go down the equity route, knowing that they could be giving up more of their profits than by taking out a loan?

If we ignore the possibility that the banks may simply be unwilling to offer a loan, there are two main reasons why equity might still be an attractive option.

Obligation

The first is that the owner has fewer legal obligations to the investor (even if some may argue that the moral obligations are higher). If the profits don't materialise the investor could lose some or all of the value of their stake and cannot demand repayment from the company. With a loan, the bank manager can simply point to the signed agreement and ask to be paid, even if you keep telling him or her that you simply don't have the money. The bank can even take you to court or force your company into bankruptcy if you don't pay up.

Therefore equity is, arguably, a less risky source of income for the business, even if it is more risky for the investor.

Added Value

The second reason for considering equity relates more to the 'x factor' that an investor might bring. Bank managers want your business to succeed; of course they do, as they want their money back and they also want to be seen as being the friend of the small business. Nevertheless, they are probably not very emotionally attached to your enterprise, so they won't go to hell and back to help the company succeed.

In contrast, an equity investor, particularly one whose money helped things get started, often has a *psychological* stake as much as a financial one and therefore needs the company to succeed on a far more emotional level. Consequently they are more likely to get stuck in and help you keep things going. They may also have skills and connections that can be harnessed to boost the company. With an investor you often get more than just cash.

Consider the television programme **Dragons' Den**. Here, businesses come looking for cash from a group of high-powered investors, but they often want a Dragon's reputation, connections and wisdom as much as they want the money. The Dragons realise this and often demand a much higher stake in the company than the business owner was initially offering, as they are only too aware of their own pedigree and added value. A high-profile investor could sky-rocket the credibility of a company, and boost profits exponentially.

Business owners have to be prepared to give up a significant stake in their company in return for that added value. The haggling over the percentage stake to be given away makes for entertaining television but the successful Dragon will then make sure that the company succeeds otherwise they lose their own money, not to mention their reputation. After all, if they force the business owner to give up 40% of that ownership, the investor will want to own 40% of big profits, not 40% of very little.

In summary, loans cost money and there is a legal requirement to pay, but the amount of debt is fixed. Equity is technically free of that initial cost but the investor's stake rises along with the profits, and so may turn out to be more expensive in the long term.

Mature companies often use both sources of finance, and you may hear people talking about something called a *debt to equity ratio*. This is a comparison between the amount raised by loans (debt) and the amount of money raised from equity. It is good practice to try and maintain a balanced ratio of 1:1, meaning that you don't end up using precious equity funds to pay the interest costs of big debts, nor do you miss the opportunity to get leverage from a fixed cost loan. Investors may be reluctant to put money into a company that has a debt to equity ratio of, say, 3:1 as they will be worried that money will not be used to fund growth but purely to service large borrowing costs. In addition, such a company might also be vulnerable to cash flow problems if a large loan was called in early.

Peer to Peer (P2P) Lending

A relatively recent entrant to the lending market, (the first companies to offer this started in the mid 2000's), P2P offers a different approach to the banks. All the indicators are that this method will continue to increase in popularity, and may well replace low value business lending by the high street banks within the next few years.

Peer to peer, or its commercial cousin peer to business (P2B), involves individuals deciding to lend their money to a specific person or business. This may be a purely private arrangement, involving anyone from a well-heeled relative through to an acquaintance that believes in your business and has spare cash to lend. Increasingly though, P2P is done via profit making organisations set up to receive money and connect it with eligible companies.

To some extent these companies are doing just what the banks do – using the money deposited with them to invest elsewhere in order to make a return, and then pass some of that back to the depositor in the form of interest. That is where the similarities end.

There are two main differences with P2P. The first is that the initial lender (the person depositing money with the P2P company) decides which company or companies their money goes to. The P2P company will list the businesses looking for support, and the potential lender can chose one or more from that list. This ability to spread their deposit across several companies allows them to mitigate risk, and support businesses that they like the look of.

The second difference is that the lender can determine the interest rate charged on their money. By declaring up front the return they wish to receive when they deposit their cash they create a reverse auction, or a league table of lenders, based on the lowest rate requested. The borrowing business can therefore choose whose money to borrow and may well get a more competitive rate as a result compared to current bank lending rates.

P2P, which is usually carried out online, is becoming attractive to both lenders and borrowers as it evens out the percentages. It tends to offer higher returns for lenders, and lower interest rates for borrowers. This is because:

- P2P companies have fewer overheads than banks

- There is competition in the interest rates on offer to the borrower

Businesses wanting to borrow from a P2P source may find the process itself is similar to that of borrowing from a bank – application form, credit check, trade references, etc. Therefore businesses with poor credit ratings should not see P2P as a softer option. Peer to peer lending companies make their money from loan arrangement fees levied against the borrowers, as well as the interest on any deposits held but yet to be loaned back out to businesses. The arrangement fees are linked to the size of the loan and are normally passed on to the borrower by being wrapped up in their monthly repayments.

For the lender, there are still some risks. The P2P market is not yet regulated or protected by statutory means, so lenders may lose some of their money if it is borrowed by a business that, despite the initial checks, simply fails to pay up. To mitigate this some P2P companies offer the option to spread the lender's money across several borrowers and have also built up their own contingency funds. In the UK there is increasing public and political support for the P2P movement, with the result that some regulation, and with it some additional protection for lenders, is in the pipeline.

There is some evidence that borrowers find the process easier, the rates better, and the decision quicker. In addition they can be attracted by the psychological contract and social cohesion of being lent money by a person rather than by an institution.

Despite the advent of these alternative loan arrangements, the act of taking a loan via any legitimate institution will place your company on the financial world's radar and its performance will impact on future credit worthiness, so again do not see P2P lending as in some way less professional or responsible.

Crowdfunding

This approach to raising finance is a bit of a hybrid, as it has overlaps with equity, loans, P2P and pure philanthropy.

The Crowdfunding process is similar to that of P2P, in that there are:

1. people with money to give or lend
2. people who need money

3. an intermediary that connects the two by publicising borrowing needs, and managing the 'dating' process

Normally web-based, Crowdfunding organisations invite bids from individuals, community projects, and businesses that need additional funds to deliver their stated objectives. Offers will be listed on the Crowdfunding website setting out what any funder will get in return. The rewards may be:

- A simple mention (in the case of a donation)
- Discounts or preferential access to the activities of the recipient
- Repayment plus interest on any loan agreed
- Sometimes a share in the company and its future success

Individuals with money who are looking to support projects can choose from the list, based on their personal objectives and the purpose/ethos of the bidder. Those bidders need to set a target amount and a deadline for that target to be reached in pledges. Normally they will receive that money via the Crowdfunding organization, but, and this is a big but, only if the target is reached by that deadline, otherwise no money is taken from prospective funders.

Therefore, unlike P2P and P2B, the potential funder does not have to deposit money in advance of agreeing to support a project or business idea. If the project doesn't gain enough support no money is lost.

Whilst this match-making process is quite similar to P2P commentators sense a motivational difference between Crowdfunding and P2P or P2B. The former seems to be more weighted toward non-financial, social or community projects, even where the money is being loaned or given in return for equity in a company. Peer to peer funding has a more overt financial return philosophy. Indeed, many lenders are making a conscious decision to deposit their money in P2P organisations as part of their overall pension and investment strategy.

This book does not offer advice on which route is best, or which P2B / Crowdfunding company may best suit your needs. Due diligence is essential and your accountant will be able to help you assess the pros and cons of the different options available.

Grants

These are non-repayable cash sums provided to businesses, normally by government departments or through their approved agencies, although there may be grants that fit your specific needs via the European Union (EU). There are also trusts and charitable bodies that may offer grants specific to your industry or sector.

Grant purposes, availability and eligibility criteria tend to vary from location to location, and many grants are only offered for short periods before being replaced or re-targeted. They are often advertised for specific purposes, e.g., to stimulate employment, to pay for marketing, or to support R&D, and so this section would quickly become obsolete if I made it too specific. Therefore I will just deal here with the main principles.

Generally there are two types – *full* grants and *match-funded* grants. The former will inject funds into your business to cover the full value of any eligible costs, whereas the latter will normally provide a proportion of the amount needed, to be matched by contributions from the business itself.

Here are some other observations.

- It is likely that grants will have specific criteria and governance arrangements, which is perfectly reasonable when you bear in mind that they are usually being drawn from public funds.

- Very few grants are retrospective so they will not pay for expenses already incurred, even if the expenditure items would have been covered by the published criteria.

- Many grant-giving organisations will only pay out on the basis of receipts submitted and almost all will specify the type of expenditure covered by the grant itself. Therefore do not see a grant as simply a cheque to be deposited after which you can decide how to spend it. You will have to spend your money first and then get some, or all, of it back from the grant agency. Reimbursement could take a few weeks, depending on the agency's payment cycle, and so you may have to use another source of funding to make sure there is enough cash in the bank.

- Most salary support grants are reimbursed the month after pay day, on receipt of timesheets and copies of relevant pay slips. These grants are increasing in popularity as the UK Government seeks to stimulate the jobs market for apprenticeships and young graduates. Your business will not attract or keep such staff if you make them wait until you get the grant funding before paying their wages.

When it comes to match-funded grants there are two common variants. The first is where the total expenditure is shared between the business and the grant agency. For example, an eligible project to design a website costing £1,000 will be part funded by the business and in part by the grant. Typically this will be on a 50/50 basis but some may work on 25/75, 60/40 or 75/25 ratios.

The second variant is where the business still has to match the grant but can do so 'in kind'. Therefore, committing the time of an employee up the value of the business' proportion of the grant might be seen as acceptable evidence of matching.

My general advice is to actively seek out local grants in your area and make full use of what is available. In summary:

- expect your application to be closely scrutinised
- do not spend money before you get approval
- expect to make some contribution to the total costs, either in cash or in kind
- expect to wait several weeks before being reimbursed
- anticipate a paper trail in reporting on your expenditure

2. Cash Flow Sources

Overdraft

Strictly speaking an overdraft is not income *received* but permission to spend the bank's money on a temporary basis. I have included it, partly because you need to understand the pros and cons of having an overdraft, and partly because so many businesses rely on overdrafts.

An overdraft occurs when a business bank account drops below zero, either as a very short term consequence of, say, a big bill being paid a day or so before some other income arrives, or as a more long term safety net whilst the company seeks to grow its way out of a poor trading situation.

Whatever its cause, an overdraft is not free money. The fact that it is often needed at short notice, without planning and preparation, will mean that banks will charge more in interest per £ overdrawn than they would for every £ of a planned loan. In some cases the interest charged could be double that of a normal loan, especially if the bank was given no warning.

Some banks will also levy penalty charges per transaction declined or paid whilst in an overdraft situation, in addition to the other interest charges. This can cause a rather perverse situation where a business is in an overdraft situation due to insufficient cash, the bank then applies interest and penalty charges; this increases the amount overdrawn and so increases the amount of interest charged next time.

Whatever our view of the banks and their motives in increasing debt by adding interest charges, the primary cause of a sudden overdraft is poor financial planning, and therefore the responsibility for staying out of that situation lies with the business owner.

Having said this, a planned overdraft is quite a common feature of business banking, particularly during the start up phase, for one simple reason. You can put one in place in advance and, apart from a set up fee, you are then only charged when you actually use it. Therefore a new business that thinks it may need a safety net of up to £1,000 in the first few months, but hopes to achieve a positive bank balance before then, might find that the cost of an overdraft is less than taking out a fixed term loan. With the latter the business may still be paying interest long after their need for the money has passed, unless the terms of the loan allow for early repayment.

I had excellent advice from my bank when starting out and arranged just such an overdraft. My income in the first few months was better than expected so I was quickly able to achieve a positive bank balance and immediately avoid further interest charges. If I had taken a loan I would have had a larger bank balance cushion but, as you will see when we discuss interest, it would have cost me more in the end.

There is no substitute here for talking to a) your business bank manager and b) your accountant, as one will let you know what is available and how much it will cost, and the other will advise on which would be best for your situation.

Interest

Our sixth source of finance is **bank interest received** and is the second of our cash flow related funding. We have already covered the interest that a business pays to a bank if it takes out a loan or goes into an overdraft situation. However, many business bank accounts have the facility whereby interest is paid to the business by the bank on any positive bank balance. Technically this is the bank paying you for the privilege of allowing them to use your money, but as we have already discussed, interest rates for savers are very low, and so you cannot expect to turn poor profits into good profits just because you have a fat bank balance. The reason I have included this rather modest source of funds is two-fold.

Firstly, if you do have a healthy bank balance you will receive some growth in the form of interest. However, if you had to take out a loan to get that healthy bank balance be in no doubt that it will cost far more to service that debt (pay the interest due) than you will get back in interest received. Therefore only borrow money if you intend to use it to grow the business. Yes, you need sufficient cash in the bank for day-to-day cash flow purposes and to guard against the unforeseen but don't simply sit on a pile of cash that was funded by a loan.

Use it… or pay the loan off.

Secondly, interest is one of the entries on the company accounts that are prepared each year (see Part 3 for details). If you received more in interest over that period than you paid out for any borrowing, the difference constitutes a form of profit and will increase the company's tax liability.

Some companies that have been successful in the past and have generated reserves of cash, might use some of that money to invest elsewhere and so earn further interest from their investment. This might include buying shares in other companies (to receive dividend payments, in addition they might make a capital gain if they sell the shares at a higher price). They might buy government bonds, (also called Gilts), which are a form of loan to the government in return for a fixed but modest rate of return. They might lend money to partner companies. Typically, the regular income generated from this use of spare cash (called Investment Income in the accounts) will be treated as interest, and will be taxed. I include this option more for information than immediate use as I suspect most new business owners are more interested in selling their own products and services than becoming an investment bank.

Invoice Financing

One of the common causes of cash flow problems for small businesses, especially if they trade predominantly with other businesses, is the time lag between submitting an invoice for the supply of goods or services and actually receiving payment in their bank account. This is often caused by offering overly generous credit terms to a customer, or by having customers who are just slow to pay.

You might think that the easiest way to avoid this cash flow problem is to simply not offer credit terms, and demand payment in advance or on the day goods are supplied. Unfortunately the concept of *time to pay* is now so universal in business that you may actually lose out if you disregard this principle. Potential clients will simply go elsewhere, safe in the knowledge that there will be other firms willing to offer the same or more generous terms. Therefore, for most businesses, a time gap between invoice and payment is just part of the trading landscape.

If you have good relationships with customers and they appreciate the problems caused by slow payment, they may be more amenable to shorter terms, say 7 or 14 days. However, you can expect 30 days to be the norm, and often much longer when dealing with big corporations and local government. One of my first clients was a major UK-based mobile phone company whose standard terms for paying their suppliers were 90 days! Luckily I spotted this before the deal was struck and I persuaded them to reduce it to 30 days. If I hadn't I would have almost certainly run out of cash before they paid me.

Had I known about *invoice financing* back then I would have had an alternative.

Invoice financing involves a specialist company paying you the value of the invoice you issue as soon as you issue it (or sometimes in stages). In return you pay interest or fees for the service. So, in cash terms you never recover all of the original invoice value. However you do get money quickly and for many businesses this can be more valuable in cash flow terms than having to wait months for the last penny. If your pricing permits you might even be able to up your prices to factor in this additional cost.

There are two common forms of invoice financing in the UK, *factoring* and *invoice discounting*, with new products and variations coming to the market regularly.

With *factoring*, the factoring company buys the debt from you and makes an initial payment, normally up to 85% of the invoice value. They then chase payment from your customer, who is now also their customer. Once payment is received they pay you the remaining 15%. In return you pay the invoice financing company fees and interest, meaning that the net amount you receive will be less than the original invoice value.

With *invoice discounting*, the financing company does not buy the complete debt, or even manage its recovery, they simply lend you a proportion of the amount due, in return for a fee. When your customer pays you in full, some of that money is transferred to the invoice financing company as settlement of their loan to you.

The main difference between the two relates to the degree of client knowledge. With factoring, the financing company will normally manage your collection activities and deal direct with your customers. Although, some do not issue statements or chase overdue debts. With discounting you remain responsible for getting customers to pay and therefore they will probably be unaware that you have already been part-paid by a third party.

If personal relationships with your customers is a central part of your brand image then using the factoring option could compromise this, particularly if the company used is in any way heavy-handed in its approach, or if your customer takes exception to being contacted by someone other than you. However, factoring does remove the task of chasing payment, freeing up your time for other things.

There is a hybrid – *Confidential Invoice Discounting* – but this is generally available only to companies with stronger balance sheets, turnover of £1m+, and a good record in credit control.

These approaches do cost money (in fees and interest),

so you need to decide whether the benefits of having some money quickly outweigh the delay involved in collecting the whole amount. A conversation with your accountant is advisable before exploring any of these options and they may suggest employing a professional credit controller to assist in faster cash collection.

There are also other bodies that can advise on this emerging area, including new products such as Selective Invoice Finance, Spot Factoring, Single Invoice Finance and Invoice Trading / Invoice Auctions. For more information on the benefits and implications of these services, contact:

- National Association of Commercial Finance Brokers (www.nacfb.org)
- Asset Based Finance Association (www.abfa.org.uk)

Double Standards

Before we leave cash flow, I need to say something about the cavalier approach used by some companies to improve their cash position. They set up their debtor and creditor periods (covered in more depth in Part 2 of this book) so they get payment from customers very quickly, whilst deliberately holding on as long as possible before paying their own suppliers. The net effect of this is that the incoming cash sits in their business bank account for longer and therefore earns more interest. I have no objection to businesses securing timely customer payments, but it is the deliberate and somewhat hypocritical policy of then delaying payments to suppliers that bothers me.

I would caution businesses about being too aggressive on this issue, particularly if they are operating mainly in the business-to-business market. Protecting your cash position by compromising another business may have a short-term benefit to you but, rather like the arms race, it ultimately damages everyone by escalating the use of more expensive lending and could lead to the collapse of the smaller end of the SME market. It's been a problem in the construction industry for years (known as subby-bashing).

Like many small business owners, the income I generate through invoices and sales includes the money I need to pay myself as a salary. As in my example of the telecoms giant with their 90 days payment terms, delaying payment to that extent is the equivalent of turning round to a member of staff and saying "thanks for working so hard in January – your pay will be in the bank at the end of April". Not many staff would stay round for that deal.

3. Trading

Sales

The final source of finance is the one you probably expected to see at the start – the money you get from sales of your products and services. Finance people have different names for this but they normally mean the same thing. *Revenue, sales income, turnover;* these are just some of the terms used. Assuming your business does well it will be the greatest source of funds. Although there are several names, for clarity I will stick to the label *sales income.*

There are a number of important things to bear in mind about sales income. Some of these will be explored in Part 2 (jargon busting) but here are just a few to get you started.

Sales income is not necessarily the same as cash received

If your business is a cash-only business, say a fruit stall or a home based cake-making enterprise, then you will probably get paid in cash on the day of sale (and you will also probably pay for the things you buy in cash, or with a debit card).

However, it is more common, (particularly for businesses that sell to other businesses, or those that offer delayed payment terms to customers), for an invoice to be raised for the goods and services you sell. Most computerised accounting systems will then record the value of that invoice as sales income on the day it was issued. However you might be waiting days, weeks, or even months for the cash to be deposited in your bank account, unless you use (and pay for) the *invoice financing* approach described earlier.

If that waiting time happens to include the end of one accounting period and the start of the next, you could find that your current set of accounts shows the sales income for that invoice but without the cash actually sitting in the bank. The cash relating to that invoice will only be recorded in the next set of accounts.

Although we are talking here about income it's exactly the same for any purchases you make. If you buy a desk on the 20th December (with 30 day credit terms), and your accounting period finishes on the 31st December, your books will show a purchase order and an expenditure for that desk but the money may not leave your bank account until literally the next year.

Do not confuse sales income with cash. Over the years the figures will probably even out but don't assume that if your books show sales income of £2,000 during December there will be that £2,000 sitting in your bank account at the same time. This is due to something called **accrual based accounting**, a term that will be explained in more detail in Part 2.

Sales income does not mean profit. Whilst this point is obvious once you know why, I continue to hear business owners quoting their turnover - "last year we turned over £1.5m" - when they were asked specifically for their profit figure. Watch *Dragons' Den* for examples of the effect this fundamental error has on investor confidence.

Sales income is the amount charged to customers or clients for each item, multiplied by the number of items sold in the period being reported. So 5,000 ballpoint pens sold during December at a retail price of £2 per pen produces total *sales income* of £10,000 for that month.

Unless you are part of the *Magic Circle*, it will cost you something to assemble those pens yourself, or to buy them ready-made from a supplier. Therefore, you cannot begin to talk about *profit* until you have deducted the cost of the materials (and sometimes the labour) associated with each pen from its selling price. These costs are called *direct costs* or *cost of sales*. The difference between your sales income and your cost of sales is called your **gross profit**. All these terms are explained more fully in Part 2.

Taking the example of our pens that sell for £2:

- if they cost 80 pence to make
- the *gross* profit on each one is £1.20 (£2.00-80p)
- if we sell 5,000 pens, our gross profit will be 5,000 x £1.20 = £6,000
- contrast that with our *sales income*, which was £10,000

You need to make a margin

The *gross margin* is the percentage of the selling price remaining after the costs have been deducted. So, keeping with our £2 pen that cost 80p to make, the gross profit is £1.20. Expressed as a percentage, our gross profit (also known as *margin*) is 60% of the *selling price*. (£1.20/£2.00 x 100 =60%).

Simple maths will tell you if you don't sell for a higher

price than it cost you to get that sale, your gross profit will become a gross *loss* and, from that moment on, you are on a slippery slope to failure. Managing the margin is an important and constant challenge for business owners. Increasing prices too far in order to create a bigger margin could leave you vulnerable to undercutting by competitors. Reducing product or service quality (to bring down costs and so increase margins) may leave your wares unattractive to customers. Therefore, neither greed nor cutting corners will work – but there are other ways, covered in Part 3.

Summary of Part 1

Businesses need money to start up, to stay in business, and to grow. In the start up phase it is common for a business to need a cash injection long before any customers start paying for the goods and services on offer.

Of the eight sources of funding I have covered, *equity* and *loans* (including P2B and Crowdfunding) are probably the most appropriate sources for the start up phase and they have different costs, risks and implications.

I also highlighted a *planned overdraft* as an alternative source of funds in the early stages but you would need to take professional advice as to its suitability for your business.

As the company stabilises and its trading activity gets into full swing **sales income** will be the major source of funds, along with any **interest** received on the healthy bank balance created by your good cash flow management. Smoothing out the cash flow waves can be helped by invoice financing, but be careful not to be so sloppy in paying your own bills that you damage your reputation with your suppliers or cause them to increase their prices in response to your behaviour.

Long-term successful businesses will be ones that are self-sufficient generators of income. In other words their growth comes from their ability to generate net profits year on year, allowing them to build up sufficient cash balances to fund new products, penetrate new markets, reward their shareholders and, in the case of companies on the stock markets, increase the cash value of their shares. They may still turn to external sources at times, e.g., a loan or inviting the public to buy new shares (called a share issue) but they still expect their core profits to be generated by strong sales at a healthy margin.

Part 2: Jargon Busting

A layman's guide to the terms used in business finance, and business accounts.

I said at the start of this book that all professions have jargon, rituals and language that help cement their status which can easily exclude the rest of us. Medicine, Law, Aviation, Architecture, Accountancy; all have terms that have to be used precisely if the profession is to practice safely and comply with its legal obligations.

When it comes to running a business, the terms used by financial experts directly affect owners. It is therefore vital that we have at least a passing knowledge of what the terms mean and what financial processes affect other processes. This means we can come to the table as equals; able to ask the right questions and then do something with the answers we get back.

Without minimising the contribution of accountants, some business owners want to be far more hands-on with the finance side of their business. Indeed many accountants welcome having better-informed clients as this allows them to spend less time explaining and more time advising.

This part of the book is designed to demystify a rather long list of financial terms. It is not going to teach you bookkeeping or accountancy. Instead it provides baseline knowledge of each term and begins to show how the various financial concepts interact with each other in the day-to-day operation of a business.

Some of these terms have already been referred to and partially explained, but this section is where they are explained in more detail. If you want to go straight to a particular term refer to the contents page at the front of the book for the headline categories.

Assets

These are things that the business *owns*. In the accounts there will a summary figure showing their combined financial value at the beginning, and again at the end of each accounting period, but you may also be asked to keep an *asset register* – this is a list of current company assets.

There are two main types of assets shown in the accounts - *fixed assets* and *current assets*.

Fixed assets

This type of asset includes: equipment, machinery, buildings, vehicles, furniture, etc.. In other words, items that not only have a useful life greater than one year, but are also harder to convert quickly into cash.

Current (or liquid) assets

These types of assets normally include cash held in the till, cash in a bank account, work in progress, stocks of finished goods ready to be sold, and any monies owed by customers that are due to be paid in the near future (e.g. less than one year). You might sometimes hear current assets such as cash and stock being described as *liquid assets* (see Liquidity later).

Intangible Assets

In some organisations you will also come across a third type of asset, called *intangible assets*. As the name suggests these are not physical items or unsettled debts, but things such as the perceived value of research and development, any patents held by the company, and something called goodwill.

If you buy an existing company you will probably pay more for it than the actual value of its tangible assets as shown in the accounts. This is because it is likely to be a *going concern*, with an existing customer base and a reputation in its market place. This is its *goodwill*. Valuing all the intangible assets, including goodwill, is a tricky business and outside the scope of this book, but at least you know what the term means.

Accounts Payable

This term relates to the value of the goods or services you have purchased from suppliers, but have yet to physically *pay* for out of your bank account. Again, as these bills are normally payable within a few weeks they appear collectively in the accounts under the label *current liabilities* (see also *Liabilities*).

Accounts Receivable

This term appears in the company accounts and relates to the value of goods or services supplied to a customer but for which payment is yet to be received into your business bank account.

As payment is normally due within a short period, the combined value of any accounts receivable normally shows in the company accounts under current assets (see also *Assets*).

Accruals

The term accrual has two applications in the world of accounting; one relates to the way the accounts are organised and reported; the other relates to how particular transactions are recorded.

First let us look at the organisation of accounts.

Accounting systems are normally run on either a cash accounting basis or an accrual accounting basis.

Cash Accounting

A cash accounting system records income and expenditure in the books when cash physically changes hands or (in the case of online banking) when electronic payments are received.

For example:

- I made a laptop and sold it to you on the 15th April.

- I bought the parts from my supplier on the 3rd April and paid online, on the day of purchase.

- You delivered cash to me on the 1st May as payment for the laptop, having been given credit terms of 15 days.

In a cash accounting system, I would enter all transactions on the days the money changed hands, i.e., the payment to the supplier on the 3rd April and the monies received from you on the 1st May.

With a cash accounting system there can be a slight complication at the end of each accounting period. If, using the example above, my business accounting year ended on the 30th April the accounts for that year would show the payment to my supplier but not your payment to me for the goods. That transaction would show in next year's accounts, as the cash was received in the new accounting period. In other words, my income would be slightly down in one year and higher the next.

As the name suggests, this method provides an accurate account of the **cash position**, not necessarily the trading position.

Accrual Accounting

An accrual accounting system records income and expenditure when the transaction occurs, even though this may be a different date than when payment is either received or made.

Using the same example above, both transactions would be recorded in the month of April, even though your cash payment to me was yet to be received by the end of that month. Therefore this method would more accurately record the trading activity for the month of April, even if the cash position was different.

The accrual system is more useful for companies that expect to have a time lag between the date of transaction and the date of payment. Typically these will be companies that sell to other businesses, offering credit to customers and receiving credit from suppliers. In other words they operate on a system of invoices and purchase orders, not just cash transactions 'through the till'.

A cash-based accounting system makes more sense for a cash-based business; one where there is little or no time lag and the use of credit terms is unlikely.

Recording Transactions

The second use of the word accrual relates to how certain transactions are recorded.

It is increasingly common for businesses to issue a single invoice for goods or services that will be provided in batches over several weeks or months.

For predominantly consultancy-driven businesses this could mean advice, reports, meetings etc., at intervals over that period. For manufacturing companies it might involve part orders or staged delivery. Similarly a business may place orders to suppliers for materials that it will then receive and use in stages over a similar period.

There may only be one invoice transaction or one purchase order transaction in the system but the effects of that single transaction need to be apportioned over the whole period in which the works are being carried out. If that period also contains the end of one accounting year and the start of another, it is even more important to record how much of an invoice or purchase order relates to trading activity in each of those years. To deal with these situations businesses use a system of accruals.

For example, if my company invoices you in November for work to be carried out during January (and my accounting period ends in December), the value of that invoice is shown as an accrual in the end of year accounts.

Alternatively, if half of that work was carried out in December and the rest in January, then 50% of the invoice value would be apportioned as revenue in the current accounts and the rest shown as an accrual, to be allocated as revenue in the following year.

It's the same with your suppliers. If your company pays in advance for its materials it can show that advance payment as an accrual rather than have more material purchases showing up in one accounting period than were actually required to do the business in that year.

You may come across some businesses that accrue their income even where the invoice has yet to be physically issued, let alone paid.

Take a consultancy firm that agrees to do work between September 2015 and March 2016. The contract requires them to invoice the client at the end of each quarter, but the consultancy wants to track its monthly activity so that it can see how much billable work it did each month. It would use a system of accruals so that September's work is recorded in the right month, as are October's, November's and December's, and then allocated against the invoices generated at the end of September and December.

I recommend taking advice from your accountant about whether an accrual system is worthwhile for your business, and how to record such transactions, rather than simply experimenting with this yourself.

In line with the purpose of this book, just remember the basic principle of accruals. They are a way of ensuring that, for businesses where there is a time lag between transaction and payment, or between transaction and work activity, the trading activity that relates to a particular period is accounted for in that period.

This allows owners and accountants to judge the true performance of a business in a particular period, so that comparisons can be made with other periods, and emerging trends can be more easily identified.

Cash Flow

A company without cash, or without their bank's permission to go overdrawn, is insolvent. As is reiterated many times in this book, it is important to understand that the term profit and the term cash are not necessarily the same. Cash needs to come into a company in order for it to get started, and to pay for essential items until such time as sales are generated.

New businesses often find that their cash spend in the first few months and years is greater than the profits they make. As long as this is predicted and funds obtained (loan, negotiated overdraft, grants, etc.) to cover this period the company will remain viable. Failing to plan for early expenditure that exceeds income will lead to the bank denying credit or charging punitive rates of interest for any unplanned overdraft facilities. Both outcomes could lead to the company going bust.

Add to this:

- the need to pay suppliers for materials, often days or weeks before getting the sales revenue that will replenish the bank account, and

- the fact that customers may not pay for some time after receiving their goods and services,

and you can see that managing cash flow is essential for any good business.

Similarly, pumping more money in, say from savings or from personal loans, without the business being likely to generate revenue from sales, may keep the cash flowing but only at the expense of increasing debt. Many businesses have gone under because all of their hard-earned profits, and more, were being used to service loans, overdrafts and credit card debt interest, and this can easily become a vicious cycle.

Cash flow management is therefore a general term used to describe the way a business monitors the ebb and flow of cash moving in and out of the company and takes action based on the information produced. Companies that ignore cash flow issues are either already extremely rich or foolish.

Chart of Accounts

This is a master list of the 'big 5' financial categories that a company needs to record and track, namely: income, equity, expenditure, assets and liabilities. Mainly used nowadays when setting up accounting or bookkeeping software programmes, the owner needs to decide what categories or accounts make sense for their business. Some software comes with a range of default charts of accounts according to different business sectors, while others will have a master list from which you deselect the ones you don't need. A few of the free or inexpensive ones ask you to create a new chart of accounts from scratch. However, even these ones will normally guide you through the process by reminding you of those five main categories - income, equity, expenditure, assets and liabilities - as every sub-category will need to be contained within one of those big five.

Once each accounting entry is allocated to one of those categories it allows a business to quickly calculate and monitor its income and outgoings.

The chart of accounts also allows bookkeeping software to carry out double entry accounting in the background so that business owners need not worry about that complication.

Debtors and Creditors

A creditor is an individual or business that is owed money by another.

A debtor is an individual or business that owes money to another individual or business.

Therefore if we are both in business and I carry out work for you in March but your company does not pay me until June, for that period I am your creditor and you are my debtor.

Your business will need to decide on its policy for extending credit (delayed payment terms) to your customers. In turn your suppliers will have their own terms and you will see these set out on their invoices and in any contract documents.

Some businesses often attempt to delay paying their suppliers longer than they are prepared to wait for their customers to pay them, in order to retain cash in their bank accounts for as long as possible. Whilst perfectly legal, this practice can rebound as long creditor payment terms can lead suppliers to fail, source cheaper goods, or gradually increase their own prices, to cope with the delay in being paid.

The UK Government has indicated its commitment to protecting small businesses and their cash flow by passing legislation to deter such behaviour. Under the terms of the Late Payments of Commercial Debts (Interest) Act 1998, amended with new regulations in 2002, companies owed money are entitled to add daily interest to any invoice that is not settled by its due date. The due date is determined either by the supplier's written or oral agreement to the period set out or, in the absence of such an agreement, by the Act's default period of 30 days. This means that even if your business never formally agreed credit terms with your customers, you are entitled to charge interest if more than 30 days have elapsed since the date of the invoice.

Remember, the Act allows a business to apply interest retrospectively but it is not compulsory that the business does so. A business owner may make the judgment that a long-term relationship with an otherwise lucrative customer is worth more than the tension caused by resorting to a legal remedy. Furthermore the legal costs involved may outweigh the amount of interest recoverable, and so some businesses may see the facility as having limited use.

Notwithstanding the protection provided by this legislation it is always worthwhile having a well written contract, sales agreement, or letter of engagement clearly setting out payment terms. Not only will this add to the professional image of your company it makes awkward conversations about payments less likely and easier to resolve.

If you have computer-based accounting software you may see the option to generate reports titled Aged

Creditors and Aged Debtors. These reports set out the value of money owed by you or due to you, categorised by the time period that has elapsed since the date of the transaction.

Typically those time periods are – current (within the credit period offered), 1-30 days overdue, 60-90 days overdue, and more than 90 days overdue.

Assuming you have set the system to your standard credit period (let's say 30 days from the date of invoice) these reports allow you to see how your outstanding payments are distributed. Armed with this information you can place pressure on your long standing debtors, as well as prioritising which creditor to pay first.

Bad Debt

A bad debt occurs when you are owed money by a customer, but you have decided that there is little or no chance that you will ever be paid. This might be due to their business failing, their personal bankruptcy, an unresolved dispute, or just a willful refusal to pay up. With this latter scenario you may still be able to pursue the matter but, once the time and costs associated with that activity have been taken into account, you may decide that it is not worth the hassle -particularly for small amounts.

Up to the point at which you decide to declare a bad debt, the amount outstanding will have been sitting in your books as part of your Accounts Receivable and will also be included in your current assets. When you declare a debt to be bad it deducts the value of that unrecoverable invoice from your total sales income. it also reduces your current assets by the same amount.

Businesses have two ways of dealing with bad debts, largely depending on whether or not it is a regular occurrence. In one-off situations your accountant will probably advise you to write off that debt after a certain period (based on what is reasonable under the circumstances, your efforts to secure payment, and the current financial health of the customer).

Alternatively, businesses that encounter bad debt situations on a more regular basis may be advised to make an predicted allowance for bad debts in each set of accounts, so that they are slightly underestimating their projected income rather than banking on always being paid. At the end of each accounting period the allowance for bad debts is adjusted to take account of the actual position so that the accounts are completely accurate when submitted to the relevant authorities. Whilst this approach is a little more fiddly to manage it does bring greater realism to the company's financial planning, especially if they are prone to frequent bad debts.

Depreciation & Amortisation

Depreciation can be thought of as being the wear and tear on an item. In accountancy terms it is the annual loss in value of any major assets, as they are used by the business.

Many items of equipment will have a life span greater than the year in which they were bought. However, the financial value of that equipment will reduce over that time as wear and tear takes its toll, or as new technology on the market makes the older item obsolete. To recognise this, a business will need to show those reducing values in the accounts.

The normal convention is to estimate the likely useful life of the item and then divide the initial purchase value by that time period, in order to arrive at an annual depreciation value. This method is known as straight-line depreciation and will lead to the equipment having a value of zero at the end of its useful life. For example, an incinerator costing £30,000 and with a useful life span of 5 years, will be depreciated at £6,000 per year. At the end of year one it will be worth £24,000, at the end of year two £18,000 and so on.

An alternative to straight-line depreciation is reducing balance depreciation. This involves depreciating the item by a fixed percentage of its current value each year, with the result that the item never actually reduces to a nil value. This method tends to be used for items that will always continue to have some residual value to the business, regardless of age.

For example, a storage container costing £10,000 might be depreciated at 20% of its current value each year. At the end of year one it will be worth £8,000, at the end of year two, £6,400, and so on. Even after 15 years it will still be showing in the accounts as being worth something as it never gets totally written off in accounting terms.

The exact period used to depreciate an asset will depend upon the equipment itself and its rate of obsolescence. A major printing press may be depreciated over 5 years whereas a laptop or other electronic gadgets may have their value written off within one or two years due to the fast pace of technological innovation. Small items of desk or office equipment will not normally be depreciated due to their disposable nature, and the complexity of depreciating hundreds of items each year.

Check with your accountant before deciding on a depreciation method as the UK Government publishes guidance on the acceptable write-off periods for certain categories of equipment.

Why have depreciation at all?

There are two reasons.

The first is to avoid a business having to allocate the full purchase price of a major item against its business activities in the year of purchase. Of course the item has to be bought and paid for at the start and so the transaction will show up in the bank statement (and its value as an asset will appear in the Balance Sheet), but its contribution to the trading activity of the business over several years needs to be recognised by spreading out that cost.

The second reason is so that the loss of value is recognised as being due to that asset's contribution to the current years' business performance. Its inclusion therefore shows the true cost of being in business each year.

Depreciation appears in the accounts as a business expense but in reality no cash actually leaves the bank account each year, other than when the item was purchased or replaced. It is simply an accounting convention that shows how much of an asset's value has been used to support the business' activities in a particular year.

Amortisation

The term amortisation has a similar meaning to that of *depreciation*, but refers to the reducing value of intangible assets such as goodwill or patents. You may recall that depreciation is used for tangible assets such as buildings, equipment, vehicles etc.

Buy, Lease or Rent?

One way a business can prevent the initial cash purchase and depreciation costs associated with fixed assets is to lease or rent some of its equipment. The items are then never legally owned by the business but many companies see this route as a way of removing the hassle of maintenance whilst also providing predictable monthly payments. In some cases there's the bonus of automatic replacement or upgrades.

The terms lease and rent tend to be used interchangeably

in business but there are a couple of important differences.

Let's say I need a photocopier for my business, but the purchase cost would stretch my cash flow to the limit, so I look to either rent or lease a machine instead.

If I chose to rent I would make a regular payment (normally monthly) for as long as I need it. During that time I have no ownership rights over the machine, and the cost of any maintenance and consumables would be extra. The initial rental period may or may not be set out and I may have to give advance notice of terminating the agreement but within reason I could stop renting, or start again, as I see fit. Think of holiday car rental and you get the idea.

If I choose to lease the photocopier there will almost certainly be a fixed period, (often several years), during which I must pay the agreed amount each month. The total amount of the repayments over that fixed period will be made up of a proportion of the original cash value of the machine plus interest and maintenance charges. At the end of the lease period I have the option to simply hand the machine back to the supplier with nothing else to pay, or settle the remaining value of the machine and become its owner. I cannot terminate that agreement without settling the balance due at the time of termination, although some suppliers will give an early termination discount.

In return for the locked in arrangement, I will normally have the machine maintained and repaired by the supplier without further charge and I may even have some of the consumables replaced as part of the deal.

This book is not intended to be a guide to which option is best for your particular circumstances; it simply explains what the terms mean. However, you can see that renting is a more flexible but less comprehensive option, whereas the chance to finally own the item only comes with leasing. Both of them differ from the purchase option in that the cash is spent over time rather than all at once although the interest payable will lead to a higher spend overall than would have been the case with an outright purchase.

If you are clear that you will need an item for an extended period then leasing may well give you that long-term security. If the needs are more sporadic and the long-term future cannot be predicted, renting may be preferable.

Please note that with either option, the value of the equipment will not appear as an asset in the company accounts, so no depreciation is involved. This is because the items do not belong to you.

Equity

An expression of partial or full ownership, typically resulting from a cash injection into the company. As we saw in Part 1 there are normally two types of equity - *owner equity* and *share equity*.

Owner equity is money that the owner has injected into the business without being seen as buying a formal share in the company. Small owner / manager businesses (operating as sole traders) tend to be funded at the beginning by a combination of owner's equity and loans from family, friends or the bank.

In the case of a Limited Company, the directors of that company normally make a nominal cash contribution at the start and this reflects their share of the company. For example a husband and wife each taking 50 shares at £1 per share both now hold a 50% stake in a company worth £100.

Some businesses are part-funded by external shareholders whose *share equity*, as the name suggests, is the money put into the company in return for a part share of any future growth.

For a publicly listed company with 100,000 shares, for example, purchasing 1,000 may not lead to much influence over company policy but you do at least own one per cent of the business. If the company does well the value of your shares may rise, so if you sell some or all of them you may make gains. As a shareholder you will also benefit from any *dividend* payout authorised by the company. *Dividends* are cash sums paid back to shareholders as a bonus at the end of an accounting period and these payments do not reduce the value of the shares. They are similar to interest, in that they don't diminish the number of shares held, but the amount paid out is subject to approval each year, and in no way as guaranteed as a fixed interest rate is.

Equity carries risk – the investor is effectively handing over some money with no guarantee that it will be returned to them. If the company performs poorly the money might be lost. In recognition of that risk equity investors normally expect a much higher return (through regular dividends and an increasing value of their shareholding) than they would expect from the safer option of putting money in a bank account.

Expenditure

Anything that the company spends in the course of being in business is classified as *expenditure*. Some smaller businesses do not make any further distinction but it is common for more complex businesses to sub divide expenditure into **direct costs** and **indirect** costs.

How costs are apportioned in your business is for you to decide, with the help of your bookkeeper or accountant. My general advice is to keep it simple and logical; don't end up in a situation where you misinterpret your own accounts and reports because you tried to be too clever.

Direct costs

Expenditure on the product or service being delivered will be called a direct cost or a cost of sales. The principle here is that if there are no products made there are no direct costs.

For example, if you sell a cake, there are some costs that relate directly to making that cake and bringing it to the market – ingredients, labour, packaging, etc.. If no one wants a cake then, as long as you have not made 100's of them already, you do not have these direct costs.

Companies normally expect their direct costs to rise or fall in direct proportion to their sales activity, hence the label direct.

Indirect costs, fixed costs, overheads

You may hear any of the above terms used interchangeably, essentially they are costs that the company would have to pay just to stay in business, irrespective of their level of trading activity. For example, renting premises is an indirect or fixed cost, as are telephones, office equipment, hire of a van, advertising, website, stationery, utility costs, etc. We'll discuss labour costs shortly, as this category of expenditure could be handled more than one way.

The term *fixed* should not be taken literally as some overhead costs might fluctuate in response to trading activity. For example, a factory that stays open later on some days in order to meet a large order will probably use more electricity but it would be difficult to calculate the exact impact on the electricity bill made by every extra item manufactured. This lack of a direct relationship means that these energy costs are normally treated as indirect, or fixed overheads, even though the reality is that they do vary.

Labour costs

The question of whether labour costs (wages and training etc.) should be seen as a direct or indirect cost is often raised. At one level it is your business and you can decide how you want the expenditure recorded and your accounts laid out. Let's start with the simple option.

If you can say that a member of staff is solely occupied on physical activities that will generate a product and lead to a sale and that, if there were no orders you could stop employing them until there were orders, then their wage costs would meet the test of being a direct cost. The wages of a commission-only salesman would be a direct cost, whereas the head of marketing's salary would probably be treated as an indirect cost.

For example, I ask a friend to come in and help me make a batch of 100 cupcakes this weekend for me to sell at a village fete. She helps me for 5 hours at £6.50 per hour, and so gets paid £32.50. Those wages costs are direct costs and so I add them to the ingredients and packaging I bought for the cakes which cost me £100 (£1.00 per cake). Therefore my *direct costs* are £132.50.

If my friend helped me every weekend, (even if there were no big orders to get baked), and did other things for the business such as help me with ordering, cleaning, driving the van, sorting out the accounts etc., it would be difficult to allocate her wage costs to an individual order. In that case it would be best to treat her wages as an overhead.

For the back office staff who beaver away behind the scenes and are not involved in direct response to the volume of trading activity, the issue is simple; their labour costs are treated as an overhead.

General (or Nominal) Ledger

This is a summary of the opening balances for *income*, *expenditure*, *assets*, *liabilities* and *equity*, changes in debits and credits during the reporting period, together with the closing balances for each category. Some software is more expansive and provides full details of all transactions per category, with the option to select or deselect the categories displayed as required. Many of the figures used in the final set of company accounts will draw upon the information contained in the general ledger.

Liabilities

If you owe money to someone you are said to be liable for that amount, and so a liability is money owed by the business. There are normally two types of liability, *long term* and *current*.

Long-term liabilities

These are amounts not due for payment within the next twelve months.

Some bank loans, as well as mortgages, would be examples of a long-term liability. In the case of an interest-only loan where the capital value of the loan is paid off at or near the end, that capital amount is normally classed as a long-term liability but the interest payable on that sum in the coming year is treated as a current liability.

Current liabilities

Where the business either expects to make a payment shortly, or the person owed the money could legitimately ask for it at short notice, these are classed as current liabilities.

With traditional capital and interest loans spanning several years, where elements of both are being paid off at regular intervals, the amount to be paid in the coming year will normally be treated as a current liability and the remaining balance shown as a long-term liability.

Liquidity

This term relates to the ease by which a company can get access to cash without compromising the value of that money. A business with high liquidity is one with either a healthy cash balance, or an ability to turn its other current assets (stock, debtors, etc.) into cash very quickly.

The issue of loss of value is important. Say you owe my business £500 but your own business is struggling and the most you can pay me to settle that debt is £250. While I can get access to some of my cash rapidly, the 50% loss in value by so doing would not pass the test of good liquidity.

For very small businesses the cash and liquidity position is quite easy to see from the books and accounts but in more complex businesses some help is required. It comes in the form of things called liquidity ratios. There are three ratios in common use.

Current Ratio

The first is called the *current ratio* and is simply the business' current assets divided by its current liabilities. It shows whether what you own in liquid (current) assets would be enough to cover your short-term debts. A ratio of 1:1 is the minimum desired and businesses with an even higher ratio tend to be viewed more favourably by investors and analysts. In contrast a poor ratio would show a company with larger debts than the cash available to pay them. This is a vulnerable position indeed.

Quick Ratio

A more stringent liquidity ratio is called the quick ratio. This uses the same basic formula but excludes the value of any unsold stock from the current asset figure. This is based on an argument that it might be harder to convert stock into cash as quickly as it would be for the other assets without seriously compromising its value, for example by being forced to offer massive discounts.

In some ways both of these indicators are based on a flawed premise. They assume that all of your liabilities would need to be settled at once and that you could liquidate all of your current assets at the same time. In reality neither of those two circumstances are likely, but the current ratio still offers reassurance that your business has a healthy cash position.

Liquidity Ratio

The most stringent indicator is called simply the liquidity ratio. It is the current bank balance divided by the current liabilities, and therefore indicates whether the business has enough hard cash, right now, to pay its current debts. Once again, the chances of all your creditors ganging up on you at the same time are slim but the liquidity ratio is a good way of reminding business owners not to leave themselves open to short-term cash flow problems.

Profit

There are several profit calculations contained in standard business accounts, of which the five most common are:

Gross Profit

This is the difference between

- the sales income (sometimes called turnover or revenue) from all sales over a given period and

- the direct costs of making and selling those goods and services.

So, total sales income of £20,000 – direct costs of £11,000 = Gross profit of £9,000.

Operating Profit

This is the gross profit figure for a given period, minus the indirect costs (overheads) of running the business together with the amount of depreciation allocated for that period. As the name suggests it shows how profitable the business operations have been.

Remember, depreciation is not a cash spend but is the annual loss in value of the company's fixed assets - major items of equipment and so on - as they help the business trade. Therefore deprecation is an operating cost of that business and its impact on the profits of the company has to be shown somewhere, e.g.:

gross profit of £9,000

– overheads and depreciation of £4,000

= operating profit of £5,000

Pre-Tax Profit

Some businesses take their operating profit and then factor in the cost of any borrowing (interest paid on loans and overdrafts) and the income from any bank balances or investments (interest received). The result of that calculation is their pre-tax profit. The reason for accounting for interest in this way is that it allows the true *cost of finance* to be identified separately and not lost within other trading expenses. In simple accounts however, you may find the interest paid and received included within those other overhead costs:

operating profit of £5,000

− cost of finance of £1,000

= pre tax profit of £4,000

Post-Tax Profit

Company tax is payable on the pre-tax profit figure and is shown in the accounts for the year in which those profits were made. Note however that the tax is normally payable in the following year.

Once any tax payable is deducted it reveals the *post-tax profit* figure. If the company has made an Operating / Pre-Tax loss, then no tax is due for that period (although the business may be paying the tax on profits made in the previous year).

pre tax profit of £4,000

− tax (@ 20%) of £800

= post tax profit of £3,200

Retained Profit

This is the amount of profit retained within the company after all of the other costs have been taken into account. If it is a positive figure, it increases the worth of the company by being added to the original value of the owner's equity or other shareholder funds. If it is negative it takes value out of the business by reducing those equity funds.

If a company is not planning to pay any dividends to its owners or shareholders, the retained profit figure will be the same as the post tax profit. However, if the company declares such a dividend the value of this is deducted from the post tax profits to arrive at the retained profit figure.

Simple businesses will often have accounts that combine cost of sales, overheads, interest charges and tax together under the heading of *expenses*, making for a less complicated report. Those accounts will tend to just show two profit labels, **gross profit** and **net profit**.

The number of profit types shown in the published accounts will normally depend on the type of business, together with any legislation relating to that sector and the features contained in the accounting software used by the business or its accountant.

It is increasingly likely that you will see the term EBITDA in company accounts, either on paper or in the language used by accountants and lenders. This stands for *Earnings Before Interest, Taxes, Depreciation and Amortisation*. It most closely approximates to the term operating profit but minus depreciation. It is a measure of the company's operating performance given the assets at its disposal, and the term is increasingly being used in businesses around the world.

Margins

You will often hear experienced business owners talk about their margins. Normally this refers to the relationship between the selling price of an item and the cost of those sales (see Expenditure - direct costs).

Sometimes the term is applied to an individual product or service (as in "I sold that yacht at a 70% margin") but it can also be used to describe the difference between total sales revenue and total direct costs for a particular period. You might even hear the terms gross profit margin or just gross margin.

It works like this.

- Imagine selling an item for £10
- It costs £6 to make and get into the hands of the customer.
- The gross margin is the amount of sales income left after the direct costs are deducted. In our example the gross margin is £4.00
- Expressed as a percentage this equates to a 40% margin because 40% of the selling price is left after the cost of sales has been deducted.

Different sectors and businesses have varying expectations of typical gross margins, with some happy to accept lower margins in return for higher sales volumes. Others may only sell a few items but the higher gross margin will ensure that the sales revenue will still be significant.

For example, baked beans are usually sold at a low margin but supermarkets sell billions of them, so they still deliver large profits.

On the other hand a yacht builder may only build 10 boats per year but the high selling price (and high margin) on each one will combine to deliver substantial annual profits.

It's the same with computers. *Apple®* might sell fewer machines than other PC manufacturers, but their margin per unit is so high they still make massive profits.

This is a critical point to understand. *Different volumes and different margins can produce the same gross profit.* For example:

Total Sales	Selling Price	Cost of Sales	Gross Margin	Gross Profit
40	£10	£4	60%	£240
80	£10	£7	30%	£240

The challenge for all businesses is to set a selling price for goods and services that customers are prepared to pay, while still giving a worthwhile gross margin. Too big a margin caused by too high a price (or poor quality, cheap materials) could lead to falling sales. Conversely, too low a price (or overpriced materials) could deliver such a small margin that sales would have to rise dramatically to compensate. There are many businesses that thrive at both ends of the spectrum – producing few products at high prices, and millions of products at thin margins.

Loss Leaders

The worst-case scenario is one where the cost of sales is greater than the sales income (a negative gross margin). Some big businesses might do this with a few items in their range, which they call *loss leaders*, hoping to attract further sales on high margin items to compensate for the temporary losses.

A sustained period of negative gross margins will almost certainly cripple the company as each sale actually takes money out of the business – the complete opposite of what is intended.

Breakeven Point

This term is not commonly used in the accounts but is included here as it is a vital concept that uses data from your accounts. It refers to the point at which the total gross profit (the gross profits from all sales in the period) is sufficient to cover all the indirect costs, the overheads, for the same period.

It can be expressed either as a sales volume figure or as a sales income figure.

As an example, if a company makes £10 gross profit on every item sold and its overhead costs are £50,000, it will need to sell 5,000 items to break even – in other words its total gross profits must be at least £50,000 before it will start making net profits. Below those figures the company will be making a loss. Once the five thousand and first item is sold the £10 gross profit on that, and all subsequent, sales will add directly to the net profit figure.

For very large companies with large, regular, and healthy turnover this breakeven point is reached very quickly. However, for small businesses, particularly those with low gross profit margins, the breakeven point needs to be constantly monitored if the company is to achieve its desired profits.

There are 5 ways in which the breakeven point can be improved, leading to better profits. Any improvement at all will mean that it will take fewer sales to meet the overhead costs after which the extra sales will add directly to net profits. Part 3 explores these approaches in more detail.

Return on Capital Employed (ROCE)

Making profits is a strong indicator that the business is making progress. However, those profits ought to be proportionate to the amount of effort put in. Some of that effort will be your time and commitment, but the rest is the amount of money tied up in the business – the capital employed.

You need to know that the return you are getting on that capital is a) worthwhile and b) getting better.

You can quickly calculate the ROCE for your own business. From your profit and loss account (see Part 3) find the post tax profit figure. Divide this by the total capital employed figure found in your company balance sheet.

$$\text{Return on Capital Employed (ROCE)} = \frac{\text{Post-Tax Profit}}{\text{Total Capital Employed}}$$

For example, let's say a company declares post-tax profits of £25,000 against capital invested of £250,000. This would mean a ROCE of 10%. Based on the UK's current low savings interest rates that might be seen as a good use of the money but only the investor can decide. Conversely a capital employed figure of £2m with a post tax profit of £25,000 would equate to a ROCE of just 1.25%. This is, perhaps, not an efficient use of capital and suggests that the company is not working its assets hard enough.

Here is a different way of explaining the concept of ROCE. If you watch those property auction shows on TV you will hear the presenters talking about yield. This is the amount of rental income per year divided by the total amount spent buying and renovating the property. The principle is the same here – the rental income after tax is the profit figure and the amount spent on the property is the capital employed. Therefore annual rent of £4,000 on a property that cost £80,000 to buy and renovate is said to produce a 5% yield (return on capital employed). Certainly better than the average bank account but it does carry the risk of that figure dropping if the tenant leaves and it takes time to find a replacement.

Return on Shareholder Funds (ROSF)

This is a similar performance indicator to ROCE but the clue to the difference is in the title. It looks at how much post tax profit has been generated from just the value of the shareholder funds, not additional sources such as loans.

This measure allows current and potential investors to see whether the company has a good track record in transforming their investments into good performance and financial return.

Sales Income, Revenue, Turnover

These terms relate to the financial value of goods and services sold, and may be used interchangeably. A product sold for £10 generates a sales income of £10 unless any discounts are offered. Remember a key message from Part 1 - sales income is not the same as profit, nor does it necessarily mean that for every sale, the cash income appears in the business immediately.

If you offer credit terms to your customers, the accounts may show the sales income as soon as the sale is entered, but it may be weeks or months before the cash appears in your bank account.

Furthermore, only a percentage of that sales income will constitute profit, with the rest being used to pay for materials, wages and any company overheads (day to day running costs).

The total amount of sales income over an accounting period is normally called *turnover,* and many businesses are asked for their annual turnover when being assessed on their size and presence in the marketplace. Annual turnover is also used to determine whether a business needs to register for Value Added Tax (VAT) (see also *Tax* below).

Taxes

There are normally three sorts of tax that a small business may need to account for. They are PAYE, VAT and Corporation Tax.

Pay As You Earn (PAYE)

If a company employs staff (and this includes the directors in the case of a limited company), and pays them a wage or salary, the company must deduct tax from the gross wages of each person (using the employee's PAYE tax code issued by Her Majesty's

Revenue and Customs (HMRC) each year), and then pay those deductions to the Government.

At the time of publication, the UK's base threshold for PAYE (referred to an a personal allowance) is £10,000 per annum. This means that the first £10,000 of personal earnings will be free of tax.

For example, a sole trader who makes a pre-tax profit of £25,000 in her first year will pay tax on £15,000 of this, the first £10,000 not attracting any tax liability. Refer to the Sole Trader section in Part 1 for a reminder of how taxable income is handled for this type of business.

Value Added Tax (VAT)

UK registered companies whose annual turnover (that means sales income and not profit) exceeds, or is even expected to exceed, a government set threshold have to register for Value Added Tax (VAT). At the time of writing that threshold is £81,000 per annum. Registering means that they must charge a set percentage on top of the value of any eligible product or service they supply and must show this clearly on any invoice.

If VAT is applicable to your business please take advice from your accountant on which items attract VAT and at what rate. The standard rate is currently 20% but some items are at a lower rate and others do not have VAT charged at all. I strongly advise business owners to seek out relevant advice to ensure that their VAT arrangements align with their business type. This is an ever-changing topic, and this book should not be seen as being your primary source of current information. What I'll discuss are the principles around VAT, rather than the specifics.

Businesses that sell direct to other businesses will often quote their prices exclusive of VAT and the invoice will clearly show that price and the VAT component allowing the other business to record both values in their own accounting system.

Likewise, if your company purchases eligible items from another VAT registered company you will find the total purchase price contains VAT at the relevant rate and the order documentation will clearly set out both the net price and the VAT amount.

At the end of each quarter (March, June, September and December) the company must calculate how much VAT they have collected from customers, deduct the amount they have paid in VAT to their suppliers, then submit a return to *HMRC* together with a payment for the difference (or a claim for a refund if the difference is negative). Many of today's accounting software programmes automatically record VAT received and paid, prepare the VAT submission to *HMRC* and then send it off electronically. However the business owner is still responsible for the accuracy of information submitted and for paying any VAT due by the required date.

VAT can be a complicated subject and different arrangements apply to different types of businesses. For example, VAT on supplies outside the UK and EU are treated differently and there are also new rules on supplies of electronic services. Businesses that supply VAT exempt goods or services may not be able to register for VAT and therefore may not be able to reclaim VAT on their own purchases. *HMRC* VAT website contains clear guidance on all these areas and will be updated to take account of further changes as they occur.

VAT Accounting Schemes

There are two main VAT accounting conventions, cash or accrual. I have already outlined the principle of accrual and it applies to VAT in the same way.

In the cash accounting scheme businesses pay or claim the VAT they have actually spent or received during the previous quarter. In accrual accounting the VAT is calculated on the value of invoices and purchase orders generated during that quarter, regardless of whether payment has been made or received. Under the accrual system the VAT amount paid at the end of each quarter could include amounts that are yet to be received from customers – this could seriously affect cash flow.

The total amounts paid over a year will be roughly the same for both types but small businesses often find it easier to use the cash accounting scheme (even if their general accounts are based on the accrual principle) so that they are not paying VAT on their sales before they receive payment from customers.

Very small businesses (the current threshold is £150k of taxable supplies per annum) sometimes opt for something called the VAT Flat Rate Scheme whereby, in return for being able to charge a lower amount of VAT on their sales, they waive their rights to claim VAT back on any purchases. This scheme reduces paperwork and could be beneficial for those businesses that do not have significant purchases over the year compared to their sales income.

If a company's annual turnover drops below the VAT threshold they can apply to leave the VAT scheme altogether and no longer either charge or reclaim VAT on their trading activities. The rules on leaving the scheme are strict, particularly where there may be outstanding transactions at the time of application, so taking advice from your accountant would be prudent if you wish to de-register from VAT. Remember that even if you do leave the scheme you will still be liable to pay the VAT component of any purchases, but you will be unable to reclaim those amounts.

Corporation Tax

This tax applies to Limited companies and is a tax on profits. Once a company has calculated its pre-tax profits it must pay tax on those profits to *HMRC*. At present the typical Corporation Tax rate is 20%.

An accountant will help you ensure that all your allowable expenses have been taken into account before your net profit figure is calculated. This will avoid you paying more tax than necessary.

Bear in mind that the tax liability shown in your accounts is calculated on the profits made in the year just ended, but you actually pay that tax in the following year. This is one more reason why you need to be careful not to confuse profit with cash.

I had personal experience of the challenges of managing tax payments. In one year my business did well and so the tax payable the following year was significant. However during the next year, business fell away and the cash I had put aside for paying the tax bill was used in keeping the business going until things improved. As it happened *HMRC* were sympathetic in considering my case and agreed a staged payment plan for my outstanding corporation tax, but it was a salutary lesson in managing future liabilities as carefully as day-to-day transactions.

Trial Balance

This is not a formal part of the published accounts but is a useful way of bookkeepers and accountants checking that all of the income and expenditure recorded by the business checks out. If the report does not balance there is normally a mathematical error in one or more of the entries. In manual systems the trial balance is done by hand, but most accounting software contains the option to generate an on screen trial balance as needed.

Speak to your bookkeeper or accountant for advice on how to prepare a trial balance or where to find the feature in any software.

Part 3: Improving Your Profits

This section does not set out to promote greed, but it is **critical** for business owners to ensure that the profits they make are large enough to make the whole enterprise worthwhile, and that any plans for growing the business can be funded.

In Part 2 I hinted at five methods for improving the size of the gross margin (the difference between the selling price and the cost of sales). The greater the margin the sooner the overheads of the business are covered and the ongoing profit retained within the business (always assuming that the goods and services are attractive to the customer and that they sell!).

This section expands on those five methods and introduces a sixth that relates to the size of the overheads to be covered.

1. Increase the selling price

It many seem counterintuitive, but companies can seriously improve their profit situation by appearing to price themselves out of their current market sector. Not for the faint-hearted, this is how it works.

Imagine that I sell my consultancy and training services at £350 per day. In my business sector the *direct costs* are fairly low (training materials, travel to the client's venue, my direct wage costs, etc.). Adding up those costs shows me that every day I sell costs me £140 to deliver, so deducting that from my selling price produces a *gross profit* of £210 per day.

My *gross margin* is 60% (£210/£350 x 100).

At this price I am seen in the market place as a low to medium priced consultant, given that some of my bigger competitors routinely charge over £1,000 per day. Some of my clients would see my rates as good value for money, however one of the implications of my pricing policy is that my advice could be seen by others as only being 'worth' £350. People often think in terms of "You get what you pay for", so if I appear to be too cheap they may infer (wrongly) low quality advice. For this reason there are some potential clients who will not engage me, however good I actually am, because they feel they need a *premium* service (and expect to pay a premium price).

It's the same principle with retail products. You could buy a camera for £250 or one for £1,000. For anyone except a serious photographer both cameras will do the job competently. Many customers will decide to pay the lower price, but others will happily pay £1,000 in order to get better quality or the perception of better quality. It's not always the case that everyone will default to the lowest price. One of my mother's favourite sayings was "If you buy cheap you buy twice".

Let's say I decide to reposition my brand, and increase my charges to £600. As long as my direct costs do not change from their original £140, my gross profit is now £460 (and my gross margin has risen to almost 77%). I accept that such a sudden dramatic hike in the price might 'frighten the horses', but for the moment let's just go with the principle.

If we assume that at my old price of £350 I was able to sell 120 consultancy days per year, my average annual turnover would have been £42,400. 60% of that total was gross profit, amounting to £25,440.

As anticipated, my new higher daily price leads to a proportion of my old clients falling away as they view me as too expensive. However, a combination of a few loyal souls and new clients who are looking for a premium service, means that I still manage to sell 90 days at the new price, 30 fewer than before.

90 days at my new gross profit of £460 per day equates to an annual gross profit increasing to a more impressive £41,400, compared to £25,440 at the old daily rate. This means an almost £16,000 increase in gross profits, even though there were thirty fewer days sold. That's a full month of extra leisure time, **and** increased profitability.

So, raising my prices has improved my margin and, even after a quarter of my clients have fallen away, I am still better off. If I chose to work a bit more, instead of taking an extra month off, my profits would increase yet more.

Increasing prices without warning, especially by the amounts included in this example, would probably not be wise. However, you might consider introducing a new product or service alongside your existing portfolio, one which is directly targeted at a more premium market and on which you could legitimately demand a higher price. Alternatively you could embark on a campaign to push prices up gradually, above the inflationary rises you might normally expect to make, so that the margins increase at a rate that does not scare existing customers away. There's evidence to show that you can increase prices five to seven times before your loyal customers leave in droves.

If you are a new business, it may be difficult to start out positioning yourself as a premium brand, unless you have personal and renowned expertise already. However, do not instantly reject the idea that high margins are greedy, or feel that you are not worth the price charged. Good market research will help you to determine how price sensitive your chosen client base might be and what you might be able to offer in the way of added value to your customer (without added cost to you). That could make you stand out from the crowd.

Not increasing your prices in line with inflation, particularly if you are seeing your suppliers raise their prices, results in an instant negative hit on your margins. Just a 1% increase in costs, on an already modest gross margin, will increase the number of sales you need to stand still by considerably more than 1%. Of course if you want to hold prices down as part of your brand offering, make sure your reduced gross profit target still exceeds your fixed costs otherwise every item sold will be taking money and value out of your business.

2. Reduce your Cost of Sales

If your market place is price sensitive and/or there are fewer opportunities to put a premium product into that arena, you not be able to increase prices, but you may still be able to increase your margins. Remember, the higher your margins are, the fewer sales are needed to cover your overheads and so the sooner your ongoing sales will be directly contributing to your net profits.

We know that your cost of sales rises and falls in direct proportion to your sales activity. In my case those costs are for training materials, wages and travel expenses, but your business expenses will probably be different. For a print company they will include the raw materials for banners, paper, card, ink, packaging, etc..

To hold your prices and still improve your margins we need these direct costs to be lowered, but not at the expense of reducing product quality so that the price no longer constitutes value for money in the eyes of clients. The ways to do this might include:

- Negotiating cheaper prices from existing suppliers in return for bulk orders, speedier payment, or continued custom
- Sourcing slightly cheaper suppliers
- Changing manufacturing or assembly processes to eliminate unnecessary or expensive steps
- Replacing hard copy client resources with electronic ones (with associated reduction in production and distribution costs)
- Replacing face-to-face meetings with *Skype / Google Hangouts*, etc.
- Improving workforce efficiency so that the same number of man-hours produce greater volumes of finished goods
- Optimising delivery routes so that fewer miles are travelled
- Utilities such as power and telecoms are certainly areas where substantial savings can be made
- ...and so on – this is by no means an exhaustive list

Only you can determine at what point the reduction of direct costs begins to affect customer perception of value for money.

For example, replacing fancy gift wrapping with a flimsy plastic bag may just pull your brand down a division or two and destroy sales. However, sourcing an equivalent quality of ribbon at a price which is just a few per cent lower will produce an instant increase in margin, one which will go direct to your bottom line profits.

Buying is a skill, just as selling is, and the application of better buying practices could have a hugely beneficial effect on a business.

3. Increase price *and* decrease costs

By now you understand the principles of increasing price and of decreasing costs. This third option combines both! At this point you may be thinking that either a) this is being plain greedy or b) customers may be susceptible to one or the other but not both! You may be right on both counts but it only takes a small change in both of these factors to have a disproportionately large impact so this option is worthy of consideration.

Here is a simple example:

- I sell gel ink pens. Each one has a current selling price of £5.00 and each one costs me £2.50 in fixed costs to manufacture. Using the terms we now understand, my *margin* is 50% and my *gross profit* per item sold is £2.50.

- A look at my books tells me that last year I sold 20,000 of them, meaning total sales revenue of £100,000.

- Given my 50% margin, half of that revenue (£50,000) is left as gross profit after the cost of sales is accounted for.

- My company overheads are £40,000, so I needed to sell 16,000 pens to break even (16,000 x £2.50 = £40,000).

- Given that I sold 20,000, I made a pre-tax profit of £10,000 (the extra 4,000 sales x £2.50) so at present I am exceeding my breakeven point quite comfortably.

Let's put those figures in a row to help with comparisons later.

Price per pen	Cost per pen	£ Margin	% Margin	Direct costs	Break even point
£5	£2.50	£2.50	50%	£40,000	16,000 pens

- I now try to improve that margin by raising my selling price to £5.20, that's an increase of just 4% (20 pence) and can be justified by the need to keep pace with inflation.

- By sourcing alternative suppliers for the pocket clips and gel ink and by seeking a small discount for a bulk order my direct costs go down to by 10p to £2.40 per pen; again that is a modest drop of just 4%.

Now lets see the effect of those modest changes, with the % changes underneath.

Price per pen	Cost per pen	£ Margin	% Margin	Direct costs	Break even point
£5.20	£2.40	£2.80	54%	£40,000	14,286 pens
+4%	-4%	+12%	+7.8%	-	-10.7%

Here are the headline effects:

- My gross margin has increased in cash terms from £2.50 to £2.80, an impressive rise of 12%.

- I now require 14,286 sales, 1,714 fewer that before, to cover my overheads; this is almost an 11% reduction in my breakeven point.

- Assuming I still sell the same number of pens (20,000), all the sales after my new breakeven point of 14,286 add the full £2.80 to my profits. My previous net profits were £10,000 (4,000 pens x £2.50) but now I make profits of £16,000 (5,714 pens x £2.80)

- My trading profits have increased by 60% due simply to an 8% change in my margins.

Hopefully you can see the power of small percentage changes to overall profitability. Watch the pennies, and indeed the pounds do seem to look after themselves!

4. Increase selling price but increase costs by less

This tactic allows you to quite deliberately shift your company into a higher perceived brand value market and ensure that your product or service continues to offer true value for money in the higher value sector.

For our example here let's take the car makers *Hyundai* and *BMW*, and focus on their small car offerings. We don't need to know the exact costs of sales or margins for either company, but what we do know is that on average a high specification *BMW Mini* costs around double the equivalent *Hyundai i20*.

They perform the same functional job of getting passengers from A to B but *BMW* successfully charges a much higher price. Part of that is down to reputation and part is due to build quality. Higher build quality is more expensive but, and here is the key, it does not cost *BMW* twice as much to make the Mini as it costs *Hyundai* to make their i20. Therefore, a combination of premium price and slightly higher build costs combine to give *BMW* a higher margin on their *Mini*.

The result? They don't need to sell as many before they cover their fixed costs and so the gross profits from their extra sales contribute directly to their net profits.

It's the same when you compare *Apple* with PC manufacturers. It costs Apple more to make each of their premium laptops than it costs say *Dell* or *Acer* to make theirs, but not twice as much. *Apple* uses its brand reputation to charge at least double, sometimes more, with the result that it makes massive profits on fewer sales. Actually *Apple's* sales are now beginning to match the PC giants, one reason why it is currently one of the richest companies in the world in cash terms.

You may be able to reposition your own business into a much higher brand bracket, take the hit on adding costs to justify that brand, but make sure the price increases are greater than the cost increases. The effect of this will be an increase in gross margin, a lower breakeven point, and therefore higher profits.

5. Reduce prices and reduce costs by more

This is the reverse principle to tactic four but has the same effect on margins. In this case we are accepting a move down to more of a budget or mass market customer base, where our pricing is mid range or even bargain basement.

Lowering prices does not automatically mean reducing profits. As long as more can be taken out of the costs of sales than is present in the reduction of price, the margins can be protected (or even increased) and the profits sustained.

This might be achieved by:

- removing non-essential features
- reducing the amount or quality of packaging
- charging for delivery
- etc.

As we know, it only takes a few percentage points of change on price and cost to have significant effects on net profits, as long as fixed overheads remain static.

IKEA use this approach superbly by providing functional

packaging, supplying standard fixings, and by relying on customers taking the items home and assembling them. This reduces the direct costs that other furniture makers would have to incur and allows *IKEA* to offer a table for £5 and a bookcase for £15, while still making a healthy margin. The modular design of their stores also helps to manage and predict their overheads, meaning that those costs do not get out of control either.

Reducing Overheads

I said at the start of this section there were five ways to improve margins and here's a bonus sixth. Reduce the company's overheads – which will then make your existing margins deliver better profits.

Let's return to my pen business, and we will use the original figures. They looked like this.

Price per pen	Cost per pen	£ Margin	% Margin	Direct costs	Break even point
£5	£2.50	£2.50	50%	£40,000	16,000 pens

We will not change the price or the cost of sales so our margin, in both percentage and in cash terms, will remain the same. Our focus now is on *reducing our overheads*.

- First we will change our telephone and broadband supplier, saving ourselves £1,000 per annum

- Next we will switch to a different utility company, saving a further £500 per annum on our electricity bill

- Instead of that ineffective newspaper advertising campaign we ran last year we will switch to internet and social media marketing, reducing our planned advertising budget by a further £500 per year

- Our overheads have now been reduced from £40,000 to £38,000, a difference of 5%.

This means we have to sell fewer pens before our overheads are covered. The revised figures look like this, again with the percentage changes underneath.

Price per pen	Cost per pen	£ Margin	% Margin	Direct costs	Break even point
£5	£2.50	£2.50	50%	£38,000	15,280 pens
0	0	0	0	-5%	-5%

Not as spectacular as playing with the margins but still, a 5% improvement is not to be sniffed at. It means that the 720 pens that we previously needed to sell just to cover our overheads now contribute directly to our profits. In this case 720 x £2.50 means an instant profit improvement of £1,800. Just enough to pay for the business owner's holiday in Barbados!

This section demonstrates how you can start to actually use the financial information and results that are contained in your accounts to actively manage the business.

Even if some of the tactics outlined above are considered and then rejected, at least the business owner is being stimulated to develop ideas, test the boundaries, and not simply file the paperwork away.

Part 4:
Company Accounts

You now know where the money comes from to help set up and grow your business, and you know some of the lingo. You are also starting to think about using this information to review your margins.

Now let's look at accounts themselves.

I'm guessing that many of you will have software that helps you to enter transactions on a regular basis, rather than simply keeping a heap of receipts in a carrier bag and dropping them on someone else's desk to sort out when its time to do the books.

Those software programs will, at the press of a couple of keys, allow you to produce a range of reports, some of which will be used by your accountant to prepare your **annual company accounts**.

This part of the book is going to look at the three most common *reports* or *accounts*, two of which will normally be submitted to *Companies House* at the end of each trading year, while the third will be more of an internal reference for you in managing the business.

If you fancy a nose around your accounting software to see what other things it can do then go ahead, but pay particular attention to these three:

- The Profit and Loss Account (abbreviated to P&L)
- The Balance Sheet
- The Cash Flow Statement

At this point you may be thinking – why does there have to be three? Why can't I just see one report that tells me everything?

The answer lies partly in the history of accounting practice and partly in the legal requirements set down by *Companies House* and the *HMRC*. Don't have a go at your friendly accountant about this one.

Each account does a slightly different job.

- **The P&L Account** will tell you where your company has been - because it is a report looking back at your *trading activity* over the last reporting period.

- **The Balance Sheet** will tell you where your company is right now – because it tells you the *current worth* of the business.

- **The Cash Flow Statement** will tell you where your company is heading – because it shows whether your *cash position* is improving or deteriorating.

Imagine you ask an architect to prepare a set of plans for a new house. Typically you will be shown a big piece of paper containing three types of view:

- a front elevation
- a side elevation
- a bird's eye view of the room layout

Each view is of the same house but each one reveals information that you can't easily see from the other views.

- The front elevation shows you where the windows and doors are located, how tall the building is and how the roof is shaped.

- The side elevation tells you how deep the house is, whether there are parts of the front and back walls that stick out, and how the roof is shaped front to back.

- The top down view(s) lets you see where the rooms are, how big they are, where the stairs are, and how the building flows from room to room.

Each view is unique, yet they are all showing you the same house. In each view you see glimpses of what is contained in the other views but it is only when you see all three do you get a true picture of the whole house.

It's the same with company accounts. Each one gives you

a different view of the same business, often using glimpses of information that will be more pertinent in one of the other views. It is only when you see all three together that you get a complete picture of the whole business.

Presentation of Your Accounts

There are a number of ways of presenting accounts, depending on the audience, and the purpose of analysis. The following terms are commonly used, but different businesses will choose to present their accounts in the ways best suited to their needs. Do not feel obliged to produce your accounts in every conceivable way, but do select the ones that are appropriate for:

- Fulfilling your legal obligations
- Providing you with relevant and timely financial information to analayse your business.

Don't choose accounting methods that tie you up in unnecessary procedures, or either over-analyse, or indeed under-analyse. Any good accountant should be able to walk you through the data to help you use it as a powerful financial tool, rather than a millstone.

Case Study - Bunn's Cake Shop

Let's take a fictitious company and assume that is has been trading for one year. The accounts have just been prepared. Let's also assume that their accountant has sorted things out at the end of the year and has given us a copy of the documents for the first time. Not good practice, I know, but let's just work through this together.

First we look at the *Profit and Loss Account*. We need to know how well the company has traded over the last year and the P&L acts like a school report card.

Remember in Part 2, I outlined five different types of

profit, many businesses tend to simplify these down to just two or three. First I will show the flow of a full P&L account and then give an worked example with just two - gross profit and net profit.

I always find P&L accounts a little dispiriting in that the further down the document you look the profit figures get smaller and smaller, as costs chip away at them. Just one more reason for making sure the figures at the top are as big as you can make them.

The P&L starts by showing us our total sales income or turnover, minus the cost of sales (the direct costs) over that period. The difference between the two is our **gross profit**.

If that figure is positive, we are off and running. If the figure is very small or negative we are in serious difficulty and need to look at our margins (see Part 3 for more on improving margins).

Next we have to take off our fixed costs and overheads, together with any depreciation of the long term assets we own and the value of any bad debts we have written off during the year. This gives us our **operating profit**.

Our costs of finance come next and we need to add any interest received from the bank and from any other investments before deducting the interest charged on any loan or overdraft. This produces our **pre-tax profit**.

Next we deduct the amount of tax due on those profits (using the Government rates at the time) before arriving at our **post-tax profit**.

Finally we deduct the cost of any dividend payments to ourselves or other shareholders and this leaves us with our **retained profit**.

Simple businesses may only record gross profit and net profit, but remember the tax liability has to be calculated before arriving at the net profit figure. For this reason it is common to show a pre-tax profit figure in the accounts, simply to indicate the amount on which tax is liable.

Before we look at an actual P&L report, here is the background information on our example business (a cake shop on the high street):

- The sole trader owner, Mr. Bunn, put in £5,000 of his own money in the form of personal equity

- He also took out a one year bank loan of £10,000 (at an interest rate of 7%) to help pay for some of the start up costs.

- Therefore the business started on 1st January with £15,000 in the bank.

- He rented a shop, bought some ingredients, leased a delivery van, and took on staff to bake and serve in the shop.

- His business is based on two types of sales; 1) general bread/cake purchases from his shop and 2) celebration cakes made on special commission from wealthy customers.

- He offers 30 days payment terms to his special customers and receives a generous 40 days credit from his materials' suppliers.

At the end of the first year Bunns Cake Shop produced the following P&L Account.

	Bunns Cake Shop	
Profit and Loss Account		
January to December 2013		
Income		
Commission Sales		10,000.00
Shop Takings		30,500.00
Total income		**40,500.00**
Less Cost of Sales		
Ingredients	7,500.00	
Wages	14,000.00	
Total Cost of Sales	**21,500.00**	
Gross Profit		**19,000.00**
Overheads		
Depreciation		400.00
Loan interest		700.00
Motor Vehicle		3,000.00
Rent		12,000.00
Telephone		300.00
Total Overheads		**16,400.00**
Net Profit (assuming no tax liability)		**2,600.00**

We can see that Mr. Bunn's business has ended the year with a small net profit of £2,600. The company has simple books and this translates into a simple P&L account with just gross and net profit figures.

Sales	Direct costs	Gross profit	Gross margin	Direct costs	Net profit
£40,500	£21,500	£19,000	47%	£16,400	£2,600

In this example we have assumed that the profits are low enough to be below the personal allowance for income tax, so as a sole trader Mr. Bunn is not liable for any tax.

The P&L account tells us that the company generated a small net profit from its trading activities. But what does that mean for the current value of the company (its net worth)? To find that out we need to see the second report.

Balance Sheet

Remember this is the report that tells us where we are now in terms of worth. Unlike the P&L account that reports on our trading activity over a set period, the balance sheet is a snapshot of the business at a point in time – in our case, the last day of the business' first accounting year.

It sets out what the company owns and then deducts what it owes in the short term. The result is the company's net worth, called *net assets*. You may sometimes see a version of the accounts that uses the term *total working capital* instead, but it means the same thing.

The balance sheet then sets out how that net asset figure has been financed or achieved. Typically this will be a combination of the capital invested, the accumulated retained profits from all the years of trading (known as *Reserves*), together with any long-term liabilities such as the capital owing on a loan. By adding together the capital, reserves and any long-term loan we arrive at a figure, the *Total Capital Employed, Total Equity* or *Capital and Reserves.* In our example we will use the term *Total Equity*.

Here is Mr. Bunn's balance sheet for the end of December 2013.

Bunns Cake Shop	
Balance Sheet As at 31st December 2013	
Assets	
Capital Equipment	4000.00
Less depreciation	(400.00)
Book Value	3,600.00
Cash at Bank	4,500.00
Accounts Receivable	1,000.00
Total Assets	9,100.00
Liabilities	
Accounts Payable	1,500.00
Total Liabilities	1,500.00
Net Assets	**7,600.00**
Equity	
Owners Equity	5,000.00
Retained Earnings	2,600.00
Total Equity	**7,600.00**

At a glance, what does the balance sheet tell us?

Given that it's called it a balance sheet there are two figures that have to balance – the *net assets* and the *total equity*. This is because the former indicates how much the company is worth and the latter shows how that worth has been achieved. If they don't balance then there are errors in the data somewhere.

The Cake Shop has fixed and current assets of £9,100 and liabilities of £1,500, making its net assets worth

£7,600. Incidentally, that liabilities figure relates to the ingredients that Mr. Bunn has received on credit from his supplier but will be paying for early next year.

You may remember that Mr. Bunn took out a loan at the start of the year so you might expect to see that as a liability in the balance sheet. However, he has paid the loan back within the year so he has no liability to the bank on the date the balance sheet is prepared.

If we add together the original equity put in by the owner and the net profits from the first year of trading, we can see the total equity figure is the same, £7,600.

So, we have a company that made net profits of £2,600 and it is now worth £7,600.

Are those figures reflected in the amount of cash sitting in the bank account? For that information we need to see the Cash Flow Statement.

Cash Flow Statement

This statement is not submitted to *Companies House*. Its main purpose is to provide information on the direction your company is heading by showing whether the cash reserves are increasing or decreasing.

It also provides a counterbalance to the P&L account by reminding the business owner that trading profit does not necessarily mean cash in the bank. In fact many companies that get into difficulty and subsequently fail do so due to a lack of cash, not a lack of profits. The two are related but not directly, as you will see from the example below.

The cash flow statement is like a summarised version of your personal bank statement at home, but instead of listing every transaction it sorts them into categories. Therefore there are fewer entries in the report but all the important information is there.

If your accounting software produces a cash flow

statement as one of its default reports you may find that by clicking on either the category or the cash figure on each line it offers an expanded sub-report listing all the transactions that make up the summary figure.

Here is the cash flow statement for Mr Bunn:

Bunns Cake Shop	
Cash Flow Statement	
January to December 2013	
Opening Bank Balance	0.00
Income	
Owners Equity	5,000.00
Bank Loan	10,000.00
Commissions	9,000.00
Shop Sales	30,500.00
Total income	54,500.00
Expenditure	
Ingredients	6,000.00
Loan Capital	10,000.00
Loan interest	700.00
Motor Vehicle	3,000.00
Wages	14,000.00
Telephone	300.00
Equipment	4,000.00
Rent	12,000.00
Total Expenditure	50,000.00
Closing Bank Balance	4,500.00

Remember, if any money physically came in or went out of the business bank account it will have been captured on the cash flow statement.

- In this case £54,500 flowed into the business and £50,000 went out. These are bigger figures than we saw in the P&L account so there must have been some big deposits and big payments during the year. Indeed there were.

- Money coming in included Mr. Bunn's own equity, the bank loan and the cash from sales.

- In terms of money flowing out, equipment was bought, the loan repaid with interest, premises were rented, staff paid, and a vehicle leased.

Let's return to that equity investment by Mr. Bunn.

- He put £5,000 of his own money in and according to the balance sheet he made net profits of £2,600 to add to that equity – a total company value of £7,600. Why then is there only £4,500 sitting in the bank and should he be worried?

- The equipment all had to be purchased with cash in the first year, but it will have several years of useful life and so this expenditure will not be required next year.

- The loan cost £700 in interest and this also had to be paid for.

- Added to this is the fact that the business sold £10,000 worth of specially commissioned cakes during the year but is still awaiting payments totalling £1,000 from some of those customers. That is why the cash received from special commissions is £9,000, not the full £10,000.

The combination of those factors means that a small proportion of Mr. Bunn's equity was used to prop up these hefty first year costs. In fact he was quite lucky as, according to the accounts he only paid £6,000 of the £7,500 worth of ingredients he purchased from his suppliers. Had the supplier not offered any credit terms the cash balance would have been a further £1,500 lower.

Nevertheless Mr. Bunn made a sensible decision to borrow in year 1, with the result that he still has some cash in the bank to kick start his next year in business. If next year produced identical income and his routine expenditure was also the same, his cash position would be much improved, as he would not have to pay out for the loan or the equipment. Those two savings alone would add £14,700 to the end of year 2 cash position.

Summary of Part 4

We have seen how the decisions and trading performance of a company are reported at the end of the accounting period, in the form of three company accounts, the P&L account, the Balance Sheet and the Cash Flow Statement. Each does a slightly different job but together they give a comprehensive picture of the past, present, and future direction of that company.

In our simple cake making company, there were profits, the net worth of the business improved, and there was cash left in the bank at the end of the year. So far so good.

The real value of these accounts is when they are compared year on year. After the second year of trading your accountant will normally prepare a set of accounts that show the current and past year side by side. This allows trends to be spotted, significant events to be highlighted and their effects on the figures understood. This can only happen if business owners actually make use of the accounting information provided by their business software and contained in end of year accounts, rather than just filing them away.

The next section of this book contains a case study of a fictitious (but realistic) company, accompanied by a full set of accounts from its first years of trading. The case study will provide ample opportunities for readers to hone their analytical skills as well as acting as revision of the concepts we have covered.

Part 5:
Advanced Case Study

Some readers will already be in business and will have real company accounts to pore over. However, others may still be in the preparation or start up phases and would welcome an opportunity to see how a complete set of company results might change over time.

This section includes a full case study of a realistic company, from its inception to the end of its second year of trading.[5]

It starts with background information on the company, its market sector, and its initial financial position.

This is followed by a summary of the operational activity that took place during the first year that led to the figures contained in the accounts.

Then we show the three company accounts together with a series of questions whose answers will come from a careful analysis of those reports.

This process will be repeated for the second year of

[5] The company and its accounts, have been generated using the *Executive Business Simulation Programme* developed and licenced by *April Training Ltd* of Frodsham, Cheshire. I am a consultant with *April Training* and use the simulation to support business training in the UK and abroad.

trading, followed by more questions, before I give the answers and my own commentary on the performance of the company, against which the reader can compare their own analysis.

Our case study business is the *Euro Car Company plc (ECC)*, supplying passenger vehicles in the Europe. It competes directly with all of the well-known auto manufacturers - *GM*, *Ford*, *Toyota*, *BMW*, *Audi*, etc.

Although ECC is much larger than the normal SME, it has been chosen to demonstrate the whole range of financial concepts covered in the book. Furthermore, the accounts themselves are sufficiently complex to require careful scrutiny while not being so impenetrable as to blunt the reader's enthusiasm for the task.

Background Information on ECC plc

ECC was established two years ago as a new entrant to the European car market.

Initial Financing

It was financed by a consortium of 500 shareholders who each bought 10,000 shares priced at £100 per share. Therefore the company is financed by £500m of share equity.

It also took out an £800m loan at the start, meaning that it had £1.3bn to spend. You may remember in Part 2 we looked at something called the *debt to equity ratio*. In the case of ECC this ratio was 1.6:1 (£800m:£500m); not quite the ideal of 1:1 but still manageable.

Capital Expenditure

It bought and equipped one production plant based in the UK (cost £675m) with capacity to employ up to 4,000 assembly workers (plus the corporate functions of finance, HR, legal, quality assurance, sales, R&D, etc.).

Car Manufacturing Industry

The passenger vehicle market has sixteen segments based on four car sizes and four customer age groups, as follows:

	Small	Medium	Large	Luxury
<25	1	2	3	4
25 -40	5	6	7	8
41 -55	9	10	11	12
55>	13	14	15	16

For example, a car sold into sector 6 would be a medium sized car targeted at drivers in the 25-40 age bracket, and so on. Within each sector there are variants, but positioning a vehicle in a particular sector does involve assumptions about the likely build cost, pricing, and promotional methods.

ECC has set a single price point for each model in a sector. These sector numbers will show up in the various company reports, which is why I have included this sector grid.

The whole industry works on average productivity figures per worker per year but these vary according to the size of car being built. For example a worker might be expected to assemble around 41 medium / large cars per year, but if assigned to making a luxury car this would drop to around 8 cars per worker per year. Productivity can be improved, as can the build quality, by a combination of investment in automation, competitive wages and good Human Resources practices.

ECC Product Line

Having studied the marketplace, and considered the production parameters summarised above, ECC decided to launch two models in year 1, positioning them in sectors 6 and 7. This placed the company squarely in the fleet or mass market for medium and large cars, a highly competitive part of the marketplace where high sales volumes need to be achieved in order to compensate for tight margins.

Margins can still be expected to exceed 25% in the medium/large car sectors, particularly if the product is seen to be of premium quality.

Operational Activity – Year 1

The following page shows a summary of ECC's Year 1 activity.

A few words of explanation are called for here. The total build cost of each vehicle is made up of the materials, designs and options cost, and the labour cost, as shown in the second section of the table. This total is then deducted from the model price on the top line to give the gross margin on each car sold. If a car is built, but fails to sell, it would show up as in stock on the top line.

In this table we can see that ECC has a workforce of 1,950 (just under half of the factory's capacity), but an average productivity per worker of 49. This is higher than the 41 baseline industry average because the company has invested in automation, training and competitive wages in order to increase productivity.

It made 95,000 vehicles and sold them all, at an average gross margin of between 19% and 20%.

Market Sector	Model Name	Produced	Sold	In Stock	Model Price £	Market Share %
6	Alpha	50000	50000	0	14950.00	1.07
7	Beta	45000	45000	0	22950.00	2.05

Market Sector	Model Name	Workforce	Materials Cost £	Design and Options Cost £	Labour Cost £	Gross Margin %	Productivity
6	Alpha	950	9080.31	2570.51	443.50	19.10	52.63
7	Beta	1000	13372.92	4407.18	518.71	20.27	45.00

Market Sector	Model Name	Target Production	Potential Productivity Cars/Worker/Year	Potential Productivity with Overtime	Warranty Cost per Car £
6	Alpha	50000	50.68	60.81	233.02
7	Beta	45000	47.31	56.77	355.60

Workforce	1950
Strike Days	3
Productivity (cars/worker/year)	48.72
Productivity Index	1.19

Profit and Loss Account – Year 1

So much for the decisions. What did their first year accounts look like? (all figures are in £m). The following page shows the Profit and Loss Account for Year 1.

Oh dear. A gross profit of more than £352m has been reduced to a retained loss of more than £51m. Now, over to you.

Q1. *What are the main contributors to this retained loss, and what might ECC have done differently to improve the situation?*

Q2. *Why might a company fail to deliver a post-tax profit in its first year?*

Sales	1780.25	
Cost of Sales*		1428.16
Gross Profit (Loss)	352.09	
Overheads		
Fixed Overheads		138.63
Stock Upkeep Cost		
Product Recall Cost		
Promotion		95.00
Research and Development		11.30
Professional Charges		
Warranty Claims		27.65
Training Cost		3.00
Extraordinary Events		
Depreciation		67.50
Operating Profit (Loss)	9.01	
Gilt Interest Received		
Investment Disposal Income		
Share Income Received		
Interest on Current Account		
Interest on Loans		60.50
Cost of Redundancies		
Factory Sale Loss		
Pre Tax Profit (Loss)	-51.49	
Tax		
Post Tax Profit (Loss)	-51.49	
Cost of Dividends		
Year Retained Profit (Loss)	-51.49	

Balance Sheet – Year 1

Now the Balance Sheet, shown on the facing page.

Remember, the Balance Sheet is a snapshot of the company's assets and liabilities at the end of the year.

We can see that the company is now worth around £1.248bn, less than the £1.3bn injected in the form of equity and loans at the start.

Q3. *What is the reason for the £52m difference in these figures?*

Q4. *What is the current state of the debtors and creditors and what does that tell us about ECC's credit policy?*

Fixed Assets	
Cost	675.00
Depreciation	-67.50
Book Value	607.50
Investment Value	
Current Assets	
Stock Value	0.00
Debtors	195.10
Bank Balance	654.26
Current Liabilities	
Tax	0.00
Creditors	208.34
Dividend Cost	
Overdraft	
Net Current Assets (or Liabilities)	641.01
Total Assets Less Current Liabilities	1,248.51
Capital and Reserves	
Share Equity	500.00
Share Premium	
Total Retained Profit (Loss)	-51.49
Total Subsidies	
Total Shareholders Funds	448.51
Long Term Liabilities	
Loan	800.00
Total Capital Employed	1,248.51

Cash Flow Statement - Year 1

Finally lets look at the cash flow statement for the same period. Remember this is a record of every completed transaction made by the business over the period, summarised into categories.

As this the first year of operation some of the categories are yet to be used, so focus instead on the rows with figures.

The year started with £500m in shareholder equity being deposited into the bank account. We can see that, without securing a loan, the company would have finished the year in an overdraft situation but it may be that they have borrowed too much. They now have a substantial bank balance (£654.26m) but the interest charged on the debt (£60.5m) is hampering their profits.

If you look back at the P&L account you will see that the interest figure is expenditure and is the principal contributor to the loss making position at the end of the first year.

Q5. Why is ECC's first year cash expenditure so high?

Q6. How do the cash receipts from customers compare to the sales revenue shown on the P&L account? What might explain the difference between the two and how could the situation be improved in future?

Q7. What could ECC now do with the money they have sitting in the bank?

So, that's Year 1 out of the way. Lets look at year 2 and see if the management spotted the main issues and then addressed them. First, what decisions did they make?

Opening Bank Balance	500.00
Revenue from Debtors	1585.15
Share Investment Income	
Gilt Interest Received	
Share Issue Income	
Investment Disposal Income	
Corporate Subsidy	
Government Subsidy	
Insurance Claim	
Factory Sale Income	
Bank Interest	

Extraordinary Events

Paid to Creditors	1174.30
Wage Costs	45.52
Total Overheads	275.58
Factory Cost	650.00
Redundancy Costs	
Automation Expenditure	25.00
Loan Repayments	
Tax Payments	
Bank Interest	60.50
New Model Production Costs	
Investments Purchased	
Dividend Costs	
Balance Before Loan	-145.74
New Loan	800.00
Closing Bank Balance	654.26

Trading Summary Year 2

Compared to Year 1, workforce numbers have increased, as have production figures and overall sales, but the average gross margin has decreased to around 16.5%.

The Beta model now has stock levels of 9,041, despite the price remaining unchanged, suggesting that market preferences are changing.

This time, are all three accounts are shown without additional comment, so you can quickly skip between them, followed by a side-by-side summary of both years. Don't be put off by the amount of figures in those side by side summaries, just look for the big trends and changes (which I have helpfully put in shaded boxes).

Market Sector	Model Name	Produced	Sold	In Stock	Model Price £	Market Share %
6	Alpha	70000	70000	0	14950.00	1.49
7	Beta	70000	60959	9041	22950.00	2.68

Market Sector	Model Name	Workforce	Materials Cost £	Design and Options Cost £	Labour Cost £	Gross Margin %	Productivity
6	Alpha	1150	9312.96	2830.48	412.53	16.01	60.87
7	Beta	1100	13715.54	4903.91	394.59	17.15	63.64

Market Sector	Model Name	Target Production	Potential Productivity Cars/Worker/Year	Potential Productivity with Overtime	Warranty Cost per Car £
6	Alpha	70000	60.43	72.51	171.64
7	Beta	70000	57.00	68.40	258.60

Workforce	2250
Strike Days	2
Productivity (cars/worker/year)	62.22
Productivity Index	1.52

Profit and Loss Account – Year 2

Sales		2445.51
Cost of Sales*	2037.99	
Gross Profit (Loss)		407.51
Overheads		
Fixed Overheads	194.94	
Stock Upkeep Cost		
Product Recall Cost	95.00	
Promotion	4.87	
Research and Development		
Professional Charges	27.78	
Warranty Claims	3.00	
Training Cost		
Extraordinary Events		
Depreciation	61.75	
Operating Profit (Loss)		20.17
Gilt Interest Received		
Investment Disposal Income		
Share Income Received		
Interest on Current Account	46.22	
Interest on Loans		20.30
Cost of Redundancies		
Factory Sale Loss		
Pre Tax Profit (Loss)		-5.75
Tax		
Post Tax Profit (Loss)		-5.75
Cost of Dividends		
Year Retained Profit (Loss)		-5.75

Balance Sheet – Year 2

Fixed Assets		
Cost		685.00
Depreciation		-129.25
Book Value		555.75
Investment Value		
Current Assets		
Stock Value		171.91
Debtors		268.00
Bank Balance		471.59
Current Liabilities		
Tax		0.00
Creditors		324.49
Dividend Cost		
Overdraft		
Net Current Assets (or Liabilities)		587.01
Total Assets Less Current Liabilities		1,142.76
Capital and Reserves		
Share Equity		500.00
Share Premium		
Total Retained Profit (Loss)		-57.24
Total Subsidies		
Total Shareholders Funds		442.76
Long Term Liabilities		
Loan		700.00
Total Capital Employed		1,142.76

Cash Flow Statement – Year 4

Opening Bank Balance	654.26
Revenue from Debtors	2372.60
Share Investment Income	
Gilt Interest Received	
Share Issue Income	
Investment Disposal Income	
Corporate Subsidy	
Government Subsidy	
Insurance Claim	
Factory Sale Income	
Bank Interest	
Extraordinary Events	
Paid to Creditors	2037.26
Wage Costs	56.50
Total Overheads	325.59
Factory Cost	
Redundancy Costs	
Automation Expenditure	10.00
Loan Repayments	100.00
Tax Payments	
Bank Interest	25.92
New Model Production Costs	
Investments Purchased	
Dividend Costs	
Balance Before Loan	471.59
New Loan	
Closing Bank Balance	471.59

Year 1 & 2 Financial Summaries

Side by side summary of P&L figures (£m)

	Year 1	Year 2
No of Units Sold	95000	130959
Sales Revenue (£m)	1780	2446
Cost of Sales (£m)	1428	2038
Gross Profit (£m)	352	408
Total Overheads + Depreciation + interest	403.49	413.75
Net Profit/Loss after Tax £m	-51.49	-5.75

Side by side summary of Balance Sheet figures (£m)

£m	Year 1	Year 2
Value of Fixed Assets	607	556
Current Assets – Current Liabilities	641	587
Total assets	1248	1143
Share Equity	500	500
Retained Profit/Loss	-51	-57
Total Shareholder Funds	448	443
Loan	800	700
Total Capital Employed	1248	1143

Side by side summary of the Cash Flow figures (£m)

	Year 1	Year 2
Opening Bank Balance	500.00	654.26
Revenue from debtors (sales)	1585.15	2372.60
Paid to Creditors (suppliers)	1174.30	2037.26
Wages	45.52	56.50
Overheads	275.58	325.59
Factory cost	650.00	
Automation	25.00	10.00
Loan Payments		100.00
Interest	60.50	25.92
New Loan	800.00	
Closing Bank Balance	654.26	471.59

Looking at the P&L comparisons, this company is making more cars and more gross profit and therefore they almost reached break even at the end of Year 2.

Their overheads seem to be going up though, and their cars are becoming more expensive to make.

In terms of the balance sheet comparisons, the company is worth slightly less at the end of year 2, due partly to their decision to repay a significant percentage of their original loan.

Finally, if we look at the cash flow comparisons we can see that revenue has leapt up, due mainly to the increased volume of sales. However all payments out have also risen sharply and the significant loan repayment has reduced their end of year bank balance. At first glance it looks like the company is 'losing money' but remember that if they don't need a loan then better to pay some back than pay the extra interest. Therefore the current bank balance is probably more healthy and realistic.

So, here are some questions to get you probing the various accounts and increasing your analytical skills.

Q8. Why are the profits not improving in line with the increased income from sales?

Q9. What is ECC's cost of borrowing and how could this be managed better in Year 3?

Q10. If the current trend shown in the balance sheet were to continue what do you estimate would be the worth of the company at the end of year 3 and why?

Q11. Why is the value of the fixed assets reducing on the balance sheet and which other account would be affected by the impact of that reduction?

Q12. We know that businesses need to have enough cash (liquidity) to be able to settle short-term debts). Using figures from the cash flow statement and the balance sheet can you work out the *current ratio* (see part 2) for this business and then suggest what ought to be done with the outstanding loan?

Q13. Taking the three accounts together what is your assessment of the general health of the company and its likely performance into year 3 if it carries on in its current direction?

Here are my suggested answers to the questions in this chapter.

Year 1 Questions & Answers

Q1. What are the main contributors to this retained loss, and what might ECC have done differently to improve the situation?

There are two main reasons for the retained loss.

The first is that the gross margin on the cars sold is well below what could be obtained. This means that higher volumes of sales are required to cover the inevitable overheads. The company simply did not achieve those higher sales as they were too conservative in their production targets.

The second reason is that the loan taken out was so much higher than needed, so the interest payments were more than the eventual loss. With a more reasonable loan the company would have been much closer to breaking even. The interest payable impacts on both the P&L account and the cash flow statement.

Q2. Why might a company fail to deliver a post-tax profit in its first year?

In the first year the depreciation on any assets will be at its most expensive, and the natural tendency to borrow enough money to have a financial cushion will bump up the interest payments.

New entrants to a market tend to be more cautious in their pricing and production levels and this means that the gross profits may not be enough to exceed all of the other overheads.

Q3. What is the reason for the £52m difference in these figures?

The retained loss of nearly £52m effectively reduces the value of the starting equity. It takes value out of the company, which is why it is so important for the business to start making sustainable profits as soon as possible.

Investors tend to be in it for the long run so are tolerant of these first year hiccups but they would seriously consider bailing out if their money continued to lose value, or was simply being used to pay off unnecessary loans.

Q4. What is the current state of the debtors and creditors and what does that tell us about ECC's credit policy?

The company is owed £195m by its customers at the end of the year, for vehicles sold but not yet paid for. In contrast the company owes some £208m to its creditors – its suppliers. Therefore it seems to have a credit policy where it gets paid slightly quicker than its suppliers do. As long as these periods do not get out of balance this is an acceptable position as it allows the business time to turn those raw materials into finished goods and be paid, before they have to settle their own bills.

Q5. Why is ECC's first year cash expenditure so high?

The company has to pay a lot of start up costs in the first year but, as we now know from our look at fixed assets in Part 2, those purchases will have a much longer life. However Year 1 is when the *cash* 'hit' is taken. A look at the cash flow statement shows £650m spent purchasing a factory, £25m on automation, and £60m in interest payments from taking out such a big loan. Remember that the value of the factory and automation will depreciate each year and this will show as a business expense on the P&L account.

Q6. How do the cash receipts from customers compare to the sales revenue shown on the P&L account? What might explain the difference between the two and how could the situation be improved in future?

According to the cash flow statement ECC was paid £1,585m by its customers, but the P&L account shows sales revenue of £1,780. That's a shortfall of £195m. Look at the balance sheet and you will see that the amount due from customers (debtors) is the same, £195m. Therefore the credit terms offered to customers mean that there will always be a difference between sales income on the P&L account and the amount received in the bank, particularly in Year 1.

The only way to close that gap in future is to reduce the payment terms but this might lead to potential customers shopping elsewhere.

If the trading activity for Year 2 was similar the difference would be smaller as the amount still due at the end of Year 2 would be matched by the payments made by the previous year's customers at the start of the new year. In real life, the revenue and cash received figures are unlikely to match up completely unless the business deals in cash on the day for everything.

Q7. What could ECC now do with the money they have sitting in the bank?

The phrase 'use it or lose it' comes to mind. ECC has clearly been too cautious in its cash management, resulting in a healthy bank balance comprising exclusively of money they borrowed from the bank. The cost of servicing that debt (£60m) is eating away at their profits and their cash balance.

They have several options, the first of which is to pay some back to the bank, thereby reducing their interest charges. Indeed that is what they did in Year 2.

Alternatively, they could invest that money in new plant and equipment, significantly increasing their production and gaining additional revenue. This is what a serious investor would be looking for – an ambitious company working its cash hard and using its assets effectively.

Year 2 Questions & Answers

Q8. Why are the profits not improving in line with the increased income from sales?

Gross profits are influenced by two factors, the volume of sales, and the margin obtained on each sale. Although sales volumes have increased significantly, the average margin has decreased. As we said in Part 2 when we looked at the break even point and at improving margins, if the gross margin goes down, even by a modest amount, sales have to rise by a disproportionate factor for the business to stand still. ECC have increased their build cost without increasing their prices to match, a sure-fire route to lower margins.

Inflation will also have had an effect on materials prices and so failing to keep prices rising in line with inflation is a bit of an own goal.

Q9. *What is ECC's cost of borrowing and how could this be managed better in Year 3?*

The cost of borrowing is the amount paid out in interest minus the amount of interest received from the bank for having a positive bank balance. In Year 2, the cost of loan interest (according to the P&L account was around £46m), whereas the interest paid back by the bank was only £20m. Therefore the net cost of borrowing was just under £26m and you can see this figure showing up as cash spent in the cash flow statement. Arguably ECC is still not managing its cash well – if it had used the spare cash to improve its trading performance it would have posted a retained profit for year 2.

Q10. *If the current trend shown in the balance sheet were to continue what do you estimate would be the worth of the company at the end of year 3 and why?*

This issue of projecting net worth is quite tricky and there is no definitive answer. However, if its retained profit trend were to continue, we might expect a positive retained profit of abound £50m in year 3 (given the £50m improvement in year 2. However the cumulative losses from the first two years (-£51m + -£6m = -£57m) would create a situation where that 3rd year performance would only restore the shareholder funds back to their starting value – hardly the result shareholders were looking for!

Also if the company continued its policy of repaying the unused loan, the net worth of the company would further reduce. All this goes to show that inflating the value of the company by having big bank balances supported by huge loans will eventually lead to a re-valuation. If that valuation is downwards, some commentators might miss the detail and just assume that this company is failing.

Q11. Why is the value of the fixed assets reducing on the balance sheet and which other account would be affected by the impact of that reduction?

Fixed assets reduce in value due to **depreciation**, caused by wear and tear as the business uses them over the years. As you now know, depreciation does not involve cash physically leaving the business so it won't show on the cash flow statement. In year 2 the assets were increased due to new automation spend but that new balance was then reduced by depreciation of £61.75m. The impact of depreciation shows up in both the balance sheet and the P&L account. If you have sharp eyes you will notice that the balance sheet depreciation figure is higher. This is because it is a cumulative figure whereas the P&L figure is just for the year in question.

Q12. We know that businesses need to have enough cash (liquidity) to be able to settle short-term debts). Using figures from the cash flow statement and the balance sheet can you work out the current ratio (see Part 2) for this business and then suggest what ought to be done with the outstanding loan?

The **current ratio** is calculated by dividing the current assets by the current liabilities (see Part 2 for more detail). ECC's current assets are made up of

- the value of unsold stock, plus
- the amount owned by debtors, plus
- the end of year cash balance.

This amounts to £911.50m.

The current liabilities in our case are just the amount owing to creditors (£324.49m). This produces a ratio of 2.8:1 and shows that the company is well able to meet any short-term debts without difficulty, but only because it has over-borrowed in year 1.

If we used the more stringent Liquidity Ratio, which just

uses the current bank balance as the asset figure the ratio would be £471.59/£324.49 or 1.45:1, still healthy enough to cover current liabilities.

My advice to this company is to secure a stronger cash position from better profits and then pay back more of the loan in year 3. It is also worth pointing out that had the 9,000 cars in stock actually sold, there would have been more cash in the bank and more opportunity to pay back that excess loan.

Q13. Taking the three accounts together what is your assessment of the general health of the company and its likely performance into Year 3 if it carries on in its current direction?

If we take the three statements together we can see that this company is underperforming. Its cash position is still being propped up by its loan rather than by strong trading and unless it takes a number of actions it will fail to deliver healthy returns for its shareholders. Those actions include:

- **Improving margins**. There is no point having good sales if the margin on each one is too low. It is like peddling a bike in first gear all the time. There will be a lot of noise and effort but little distance travelled.

- **Sorting out the unsold stock**. This situation is telling the company that there are people who don't like the complete package of price and features. Unless this is addressed sales and profits will fall as more stock remains unsold.

- **Making better use of the assets**. There is a factory capable of taking 4000 workers (with the fixed overheads to match) but there are only 2250 workers in it. Unless their productivity further improves those overheads will continue to eat away at the modest gross profits being obtained.

- **Stopping paying more in loan interest than the bank is paying back**. To have a loan and not use it is simply giving money away. Investors don't like money that they provided being used to pay debt interest and it can lead to some spicy boardroom discussions.

Conclusion

Running a business is a serious affair. Get it right and the rewards are considerable; get it wrong and the penalties can be severe. There are a lot of terms and numbers in this book and, despite my best efforts to make it understandable to a lay-person, you may still flick through a few pages and declare "No, too many sums for my liking!"

However, the figures themselves are just consequences of business decisions, and the various accounts are just tools to help you run the business more effectively. Turning a blind eye to business finance will lead to two outcomes:

1. The business might succeed and you will never really know why, or
2. The business will fail and you will never really know why.

Obviously, the second outcome is more damaging but failing to learn from what does work should also be avoided where possible, otherwise you will miss opportunities to be even more successful.

Here is a short, if somewhat carnivorous, parable that explains this concept beautifully.

An isolated tribe lived in grass huts in the jungle, eating mainly vegetables and boiled pork from the pigs they kept around the village. Sometimes they kept the pigs in the huts for safety.

One day, whilst the tribe was out hunting, a spark from the fire set one of the grass huts alight, unfortunately roasting the sheltering pig. The tribe returned and were transfixed by this new and exciting aroma. As you might imagine they set upon devouring the carcass and generally agreed that they had found their new staple diet.

A few weeks, and many pigs later, they ran out of huts!

Their failure to understand how this new food source had occurred led to them simply replicating the original conditions – a pig in a grass hut, set alight. Had they broadened their thinking they might have found alternative ways to achieve the same end result without destroying their housing stock! Vegetarian and vegan readers can re-engage now.

It's the same with running a business that is doing OK; unless you know why and can explore ways to maximize that success you risk triggering unintentional consequences. These are the things that make one thing better, but which accidentally damage another part of the business. Some examples of this phenomenon include:

- Increasing volumes of production/sales instead of looking to increase margins. The profits might go up for a while but the consequences are that staff become stressed, equipment fails more frequently, and cash flow is compromised due to more regular purchases of materials. Eventually the profit benefits are eaten away by higher costs and lost productivity... and the bubble bursts.

- Borrowing to achieve a healthy bank balance, but then not using that money to drive growth. This was the problem for our case study earlier and shows the problem of fixating on one part of the business finance system to the exclusion of the others.

- (For larger companies) paying generous dividends as soon as profits have been generated. Whilst this might appear to keep investors on side, it must be remembered that most of them gave you the money for long-term growth. A modest dividend might help to keep them sweet but simply giving them back large chunks of their own money means it is not available to drive growth. It also means that they might have been better advised to keep the money in their bank account, with lower returns but also lower risk, or to find a more growth-oriented company in which to invest.

All of those behaviours make sense if you only see part of the business. This book allows you to see the **whole system**, to analyse how a decision made in one part of the business has knock on effects in other parts. As you are now only too aware, virtually every decision taken within a business will have a financial consequence and it is within the accounts that those consequences can be found.

This book has shown you:

- How to get your hands on the money
- What labels are attached to that money once it is bouncing round your business
- How the company accounts are assembled
- What messages they contain

As a result, you are now in a much better position to truly *manage* your business and not just be *in* business.

6917161R10084

Printed in Germany
by Amazon Distribution
GmbH, Leipzig